the angel book

the angel book

Vanessa Lampert

CICO BOOKS
London New York

Published in 2007 by
CICO Books
an imprint of Ryland, Peters & Small Ltd
519 Broadway, 5th Floor
New York, NY 10012
Copyright © CICO Books Ltd 2007

www.cicobooks.co.uk

Text copyright © Vanessa Lampert 2007
Design and illustration copyright © CICO Books 2007

The right of Vanessa Lampert to be identified as the author
of this work has been asserted by her in accordance with the
Copyright, Designs and Patents Act 1988.

All rights reserved. No part of this publication may be
reproduced, stored in or introduced into a retrieval system,
or transmitted in any form or by any means, electronic,
mechanical, photocopying, recording or otherwise, without the
prior written permission of the copyright holder and publisher.

10 9 8 7 6 5 4 3 2 1

A CIP catalog record for this book is available from the Library
of Congress.

ISBN-10: 1 906094 17 9
ISBN-13: 978 1 906094 17 1

Printed in China

Editors Samantha Gray and Marie Clayton
Designer Claire Legemah
Illustrator Emma Garner

When someone invites their Angels to convers

Contents

with them, all the Angelic Hierarchies rejoice

PART 1

Discovering
Angels

By connecting with the Angelic and spiritual realms we bring love and compassion into our lives.

Adoration of an Angel, *Fra Angelico, 1420s, panel, Louvre, Paris, France.*

What are Angels?

The word "Angel" comes from the Greek "angelos," which means "messenger." The corresponding Hebrew word is mal'ak, which has the same meaning. Angels bridge the gap between our physical world and the Cosmos, or Universe. They are God's messengers and intermediaries, conveying His wishes to humankind but also available to guide, protect, and teach us.

Many believe that God created all Angels simultaneously on the second day of Creation with the exception of Metatron and Sandalphon—reputedly the prophets Enoch and Elijah who became Angels when they ascended to Heaven.

Angels are spirits of pure energy and often appear as rays of light, although religious texts describe them in a number of ways. They are androgynous, but often take on the appearance of men. In Genesis 18, for example, Abraham welcomes three Angelic guests who at first seem to be travelers. In the next chapter Angels appear again as men, when they visit Job in Sodom. Thus most of the familiar Angels have male names. It is not until the Jews are exiled to Babylon that there are descriptions of Angels with wings. Some even take on a more frightening appearance as in the Book of Ezekiel (1:5–13 and 10:10–14).

Afro-Caribbean angel

ANGELS AND SPIRITUAL GUIDES

God created Angels before humankind. Spiritual guides, on the other hand, were once people living on Earth who have chosen to help us either through guidance or through healing energies.

The Annunciaton, *Hans Multscher, 1458, oil on panel, Museo Multscher, Vipiteno, Italy.*

Where Angels Tread

Humankind has always believed in Angels. They play a major role in world religions, and religions texts are fascinating guides to the Angelic realms. While most agree that Angels are the messengers and servants of God, each religions tradition contributes fresh insights into how Angels connect with us. A deeper understanding will enhance your spiritual practice.

ZOROASTRIANISM

Zoroastrianism is one of the world's oldest religions, originating in what is now Iran. It is based on the teachings of the prophet Zoroaster, also called Zarathushtra or Zartosht (around 1400 BCE to 1000 BCE).

Central to Zoroastrianism is the battle between light and dark, good and evil. The opposing forces in this battle are Ahura Mazda (God) and his evil antithesis, Angra Mainya (the Devil). Their followers are the Angelic ahuras and the demonic daevas. Zoroaster tells us that Ahura Mazda created the Universe using aspects of the Creator known as the Amesha Spentas. These were mythologized into Angelic Hierarchies.

Amesha Spentas (Archangels) Literally "Beneficent Immortals," these are the highest spiritual beings created by Ahura Mazda.

Fravashis (Guardian Angels) Each person, through life, is accompanied by a guiding Angel. Guardian Angels are also known as Arda Fravash (Holy Guardian Angels).

Yazatas (Adorable Ones) These spiritual beings are created to help people and to protect them from evil.

JUDAISM

A number of spiritual beings subordinate to God appear throughout the *Old Testament*. There are the Malach (Messenger Angels),

the Irinim (Watchers/High Angels), Cherubim (Mighty Ones), Sarim (Princes), Seraphim (Fiery Ones), Chayyot (Holy Creatures), and Ofanim (Wheels). In some biblical accounts spiritual beings are indistinguishable from human beings, while in others their appearance varies—for instance, *Ezekiel 1:6* and *10:21* describes them as having four faces and four wings.

Collective terms for Angels include Tzeva (Host), B'nei ha-Elohim or B'nai Elim (Sons of God), Kedoshim (Holy Ones), and Adat El (Divine Assembly). In the *Old Testament* only

Jacob's Dream of the Ladder, *Matthaus the Elder, 1625, copperplate engraving.*

three Angels are named: Michael, Gabriel, and Satan. However, other Angels often appear—for example, Jacob's vision of Angels ascending and descending to Heaven, the warning to Lot, and the Angels found in the *Book of Ezekiel*.

Biblical Angels have a variety of roles, including protecting, rescuing and advising human beings. The *Book of Daniel* describes Michael as Israel's representative in Heaven, with other nations also represented by Angelic princes. It also states that there are Angelic Hierarchies, and that each of us has a Guardian Angel who is with us for our lives.

Angels also often appear in apocryphal literature—the books written by ancient Jews that were not made part of the *Bible*, including the *Books of the Maccabees* and the *Books of Enoch*. The "Manual of Discipline," part of the *Dead Sea Scrolls*, speaks of an Angel of Light and an Angel of Darkness.

Most Jewish folklore sees Angels as guardians. Their names are printed on amulets to protect the innocent against demons. An old tradition (*Talmud, Shabbat 119b*) teaches that two Angels, one good and one bad, follow people home on a Shabbat (weekly day of rest). If all is prepared—the challah (traditional bread), wine, and candles—the good Angel exclaims, "May it be thus on another Sabbath too," and the evil Angel responds unwillingly "Amen." If the house is not prepared the evil Angel exclaims, "May it even be thus on another Sabbath too," and the good Angel must respond "Amen."

Angel of Light–Dark

THE KABBALAH

The Kabbalah is one of the richest sources of Angelic lore. According to Kabbalist writings Angels were created before the Earth was made, at the point when God said "Let there be light." Angels were used in the creation of human beings but then became envious of their free will. There are good and bad Angels in the Angelic realms; *Fallen Angels* (see page 34) are seen as negative messengers, rather than being evil. Some of the main Angels mentioned in the Kabbalah are Michael, Gabriel, Uriel, Raphael, and Sandalphon (see *Angels & Kabbalah*, page 16). Lilith is the Angel of the Night and is considered by many to be the arch she-devil (see *Lilith*, pages 22–23).

CHRISTIANITY

Angels are prominent in Christian beliefs and appear frequently as the ministers and messengers of God. The Archangel Gabriel, for example, announces the birth of St John the Baptist to Elizabeth, and announces to Mary that she will bear the Messiah and that she is to call him Jesus.

Throughout the *New Testament* it is implied that each individual soul has a Guardian or protecting Angel, for example:

Mikael, Angel of Rain

Take heed that ye despise not one of these little ones; for I say unto you, That in heaven their Angels do always behold the face of my Father, which is in Heaven.

MATTHEW 18:10, KING JAMES BIBLE

The Catholic Church follows the principal of the Hierarchy (or Choirs) of Angels (see page 26), and the most important Angels are the Archangels Gabriel, Michael and Raphael. Catholicism views Angels as God's instruments of communication and encourages its devotees to pray for Angelic help. Some Protestant theologians, on the other hand, discourage praying to Angels.

ISLAM

Belief in Angels is one of the fundamental articles of faith in Islam. The Arabic word for Angel is malak (plural mala'ikah), meaning "messenger." Muslims believe that the Angel Gabriel—or Jibril— was the messenger through whom God (Allah) revealed the *Koran* (*Qur'an*) to the Prophet Mohammed.

Islamic Angels

Islam teaches that Angels are created from light and are invisible. They do not have free will but are completely devoted to serving God, carrying out all His commands without question. Angels belong to a level of existence beyond the perceptible world, which is called alam al-ghayb (world of the unseen). They are described as being excessively beautiful in appearance, with different numbers of wings.

Muslims believe that people have two Guardian Angels : Raqeeb sits on your right shoulder and records all your good deeds; Ateed sits on your left shoulder and records all your bad deeds.

The full number of Angels is only known to God, but Angels familiar to people are:

Jibril (Jibrail, Jibraaiyl, Jibreel, or Gabriel in English and the *Bible*) is known for conveying God's revelations and messages to the Muslim prophets.

Mikail (Mikaaiy, Mikaeel, or Michael) is the Archangel responsible for rain over the Earth, sending it wherever God wishes. He has helpers to assist him in directing the winds and clouds, and he oversees the cultivation of crops on Earth.

Israfil (Israafiyl, Israfeel, or Raphael) is the Angel responsible for signaling the coming of Judgment Day by blowing a horn and sending out a "Blast of Truth." He will also be responsible for the Resurrection of all accountable beings to face Judgment Day.

Azrael is the Angel of Death who, with his helpers, is responsible for parting the soul from the physical body. If a person has led a bad life, the soul is ripped out very painfully, but a righteous person's soul is separated like a "drop of water dripping from a glass." Other named Angels include:

Maalik is responsible for Hell (Jahannum).

Ridwan is responsible for Heaven (Paradise or Jannah).

Nakir and Munkar the Angels who question the dead in their graves on issues relating to their God, religious beliefs, deeds, etc.

BUDDHISM

Buddhism is also known as Buddha Dharma or Dhamma, which means the "teachings of the Awakened one," and was founded around the 5th century BCE by Siddhartha Gautama. The Buddhist equivalent to Angels are Devas (celestial beings). Some schools of Buddhism also refer to Dharmapalas (Dharma protectors). In Tibetan Buddhism, Devas are sometimes considered to be the emanations of Bodhisattvas (enlightened beings). Different schools of Buddhism have various Devas who do not normally interfere with human affairs.

However, in Thailand it is believed that Devas approve of people who meditate and will harass people who do not behave properly.

THE LATTER DAY SAINTS MOVEMENT

Mormonism is a term used to describe the ideology of the Latter Day Saints Movement, founded by Joseph Smith (1805–1844) in 1830. Mormon was an ancient American prophet, born sometime between 350–365 CE, who compiled the records of his people on gold plates. He gave these to his son, Moroni, and they were buried in what is now New York State.

In 1823, Moroni appeared to Joseph Smith as an Angel, giving him details about the ancient records and instructing him about their translation into English. Joseph Smith describes his first Angelic encounter in *Joseph Smith History 1:30–47*. Between the years 1823 and 1829 Angel Moroni appeared to him repeatedly. In 1827 Joseph Smith retrieved the plates and translated them into the *Book of Mormon*, published in 1830.

Mormons believe that people can be baptized after death and that human beings can become gods in the afterlife. Joseph Smith is viewed as a prophet of God.

Angels & Kabbalah

Kabbalah is the mystical aspect of Judaism, an esoteric system of interpreting the Old Testament, Jewish scriptures, and other sacred writings. It is based on the belief that every letter, word, number—and in some cases sound—contains the mysteries of creation.

Kabbalah is a treasure house of Angelic lore. The word "Kabbalah" comes from the Hebrew "to receive" and refers to a secret oral tradition of teaching. Kabbalah includes not only religious and philosophical teachings, but also magic and mysticism.

There is no one book that contains all there is to know about Kabbalah, which is intertwined with Jewish folklore. The main Kabbalah texts are the *Zohar* (*Book of Splendor*), dating from the 13th century CE, and the *Sepher Yetzirah* (*Book of Creation or Formation*), probably written in the 2nd century CE.

It is thought that the Archangel Raziel, the "Keeper of Secrets" who stands close to the

Angel Raziel

throne of God, writes down everything he hears discussed. He gave the *Sepher Raziel HaMalach* (*Book of Raziel the Angel*), said to be the first book ever written, to Adam and Eve after they were expelled from the Garden of Eden, so that they could learn to understand God better and find their way "home."

The book was then passed on through generations to Enoch, before the Archangel Raphael gave it to Noah who used its wisdom to build the Ark.

There are two main mystical aspects of Kabbalah. These are the ma'aseh bereishit—the work of Creation based on the Tree of Life—and ma'aseh Merkavah—the work of the chariot.

The Prophet Enoch, *Turkish miniature, 16th century, Topkapi Museum, Istanbul, Turkey.*

ANGELS AND THE TREE OF LIFE

Kabbalists use the symbol of the Tree of Life to demonstrate the link between the physical world and the Cosmos. The Tree is seen as a representation of the Universe and of every being living in it, together with their place in the order of things. The basic Tree is a representation only of our immediate terrestrial world. Kabbalah teaches us that there are three higher worlds above this, each represented by another Tree, with the spheres overlapping one another. In order to ascend back to our original place in the Cosmos from whence we came before birth, we must learn to climb back up the Tree spiritually, step by step, layer by layer.

The Tree contains 10 centers, or spheres, called Sephirot, which are usually illustrated in three distinct columns. Between each of the 10 Sephirot run 22 channels, or pathways, which connect them. Each channel is assigned a letter of the Hebrew alphabet and each Hebrew letter is also a number— Aleph, the first letter, is number one. The link between the letters of the Hebrew alphabet, their sounds, and their numerical energy, is extremely important. Kabbalists believe that the Hebrew alphabet existed before Creation and that its sounds, numerical equivalents

(called gemetria), forms, and positions are the physical expression of God's divine energy. The 22-letter alphabet was thus the basis for the Creation.

All the Sephirot emanate from God and the Cosmos. Although originally formed of pure, clear Divine energy, as they descend to the physical world they take on various colors and forms. A Sephirah (singular) is usually envisioned as a circle, and all the circles of Sephirot are linked to each other to form a symbol that represents the totality of Creation. Each Sephirah has its own individual energy and property. The higher Trees are said to be the habitations of Angels. Each Tree is assigned an Archangel to watch over it and to help those who are working spiritually to ascend through it.

The highest entities of the Angelic world are the Holy Spirits of the inner council, under the leadership of Metatron who resides at Kether, the Crown of the Universe. On the central pillar, the Archangels Michael and Gabriel hold special roles in relation to humankind, because they are the vehicles through which Metatron communicates to Sandalphon at the level of Malkhut. Malkhut represents Kingdom, which is the physical world where humankind exists.

Tree of Life

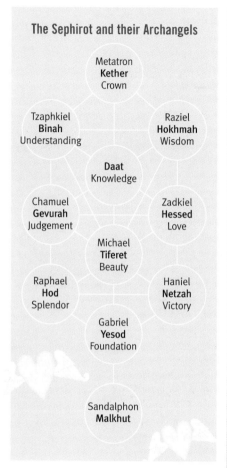

The Sephirot and their Archangels

Metatron
Kether
Crown

Tzaphkiel
Binah
Understanding

Raziel
Hokhmah
Wisdom

Daat
Knowledge

Chamuel
Gevurah
Judgement

Zadkiel
Hessed
Love

Michael
Tiferet
Beauty

Raphael
Hod
Splendor

Haniel
Netzah
Victory

Gabriel
Yesod
Foundation

Sandalphon
Malkhut

Study of Kabbalah can be divided into three aspects. The term Theoretical Kabbalah is often given to the study of the hidden meanings contained in holy texts and writings. Meditative Kabbalah explores ways of communicating with God through meditation and prayer. Practical Kabbalah ranges from self-help programs to mystical aspects such as wearing red wool on the wrist to protect against negative energies. Its main purpose is to connect with our souls and eventually to form open channels with the Cosmos.

ANGELS AND MERKAVAH MYSTICISM

Merkavah (Hebrew for "chariot") is an early form of Jewish mysticism dating from circa 600 CE. The main source of writing about Merkavah comes from a Hebrew text *Hekhalot Rabbati* (*The Greater Heavenly Halls*). Merkavah Mysticism aims to recreate the ecstatic vision seen by the Prophet Ezekiel and described in *Ezekiel Chapters 1–3*. Central to this vision was the Chariot of God drawn by the four Holy Living Creatures.

The process, as laid down in the *Herkhalot Rabbati*, describes the mystic traveling out of the body through Seven Chambers, one inside the other. At the door to each Chamber are Angelic Guardians, whom the mystic must appease before being allowed to continue the journey. The Seven Chambers represent seven levels of purity and holiness and, to accomplish the journey, the mystic must succeed in raising energy levels sufficiently each time the next Chamber is reached. The ultimate goal is to enter the Seventh Chamber, where the mystic can behold the same vision as Ezekiel, complete with Angels and the throne of God. In order to commence the Merkavah journey, the mystic must call upon Surayah, The Prince of Countenance (a title of Metatron) for help.

Before each Chamber can be entered, the Angels guarding the doorways must be shown the Archangelic Seal of Surayah.

The Seven Chambers of Merkavah

ANGELS AND PROTECTION

Kabbalist manuscripts often give instructions for the preparation of amulets with the names of Angels inscribed on them. It Is usually specified that the amulet can only be inscribed by a God-fearing person who has been trained in Kabbalah. An example is contained in a Yemenite remedy book, which was written in Hebrew in the 19th century but most certainly copied from earlier sources. .

In the instructions for making an amulet for a pregnant woman the scribe is told to write the names of the Angels Michael, Gabriel, Chamuel, and Raphael, who guard the baby in the womb, and to make a blessing over it. The parchment would then be rolled up for the Yemenite Jewish woman to carry in an amulet until her pregnancy reached full term. Probably among the most well-known amulets are those that protect babies from Lilith.

The story of Lilith

I love the story of Lilith because, although she is portrayed by many as a powerful she-devil, others—including myself—believe that she was, in fact, the world's first feminist. The legend of Lilith is first mentioned in a work called the *Alphabet of Ben-Sira*, written around 600–1000 CE. This explores the belief that Eve was not Adam's first wife but his second. Lilith, like Adam, was created from the dust of the Earth but they quarreled and never found peace together. Adam expected her to be completely submissive and obedient to his wants and wishes, but unfortunately for him Lilith believed that—since they were both created from the same source—they were both equal and she refused to be subservient. One of the main bones of contention was that she refused to lie beneath him in intercourse:

Adam and Lilith began to fight. She said:

"will not lie below," and he said, "I will not lay beneath you, but only on top. For you are fit only to be in the bottom position, while I am the superior one."

Alphabet of Ben-Sira

Because Adam tried to force her to obey, Lilith spoke the magical name of God and left him. Adam then prayed to God, asking Him to help bring her back. Three Angels, Sanvai, Sansanvai, and Semanglof, were dispatched to fetch her and God ordered them to tell her that, if she refused to obey His commands, 100 of her offspring would die daily. The three Angels followed Lilith to the Red Sea and told her God's warning but she refused to return. They threatened to drown her, but she answered that she had been created for the purpose of punishing young infants. She said that she had power over them from the day that they were born until they were eight days old if they were boys (this is when boys are usually circumcised) and until the 20th day if they were girls. Hearing this the three Angels wished to drown her, but she begged them to let her live and they agreed.

Lilith

However, she swore to them in the name of the Lord that if she saw the names, images, or faces of the three Angels upon an amulet in any room where there was a baby, she would not touch it. The Sefer Raziel describes the formula to be written upon an amulet or a piece of paper. Even today, the protective written formula is sometimes placed in the rooms of newborn babies. It refers to Lilith as the first Eve and, in the name of the Angels Sanvai, Sansanvai, and Semanglof, conjures her not to harm the babies in whose rooms she finds the amulet or piece of paper.

Further writings on this legend give a number of different versions of what happens to Lilith next. In some she becomes the Queen of the Demons, while in others she is married to Samael—who is believed to be the Devil. She is accompanied by 408 hosts of evil spirits and destroying Angels.

THE ANGELS OF ENOCH

The *Books of Enoch* are one of the richest sources of Angelic lore. Enoch was a prophet who is thought to have lived around 3284–3017 BCE, and was the son of Jared and the great-grandfather of Noah. He is one of the two people in the *Bible* taken up to Heaven while still alive:

> *And Enoch walked with God: and he was not; for God took him.*
> **GENESIS 5:24, KING JAMES BIBLE**

Although Enoch is the supposed author of 366 books, which are collectively termed Enochian literature, the most famous of his writings are normally referred to as the *First*, *Second,* and *Third Books of Enoch*.

First Book of Enoch also known as the "Ethiopic Book of Enoch" because the only full surviving manuscript is in Ethiopic. This is considered the most important of the *Books* and anyone referring to the "Book of Enoch" normally means this one.

Second Book of Enoch also known as the "Slavonic Book of Enoch" because the only known existing manuscript is a Slavonic translation of the original Greek text. Although in some ways similar to the *First Book of Enoch*, it details Enoch's journey through the Seven Heavens, predicts the Great Flood, and contains descriptions of Angels residing in Heaven.

been buried around 70 BCE.

The *First Book of Enoch* consists of five distinct sections:

Book of Watchers This describes the Fall of the Angels, the Dream Vision of Enoch, and his intercession for Azazel and the Fallen Angels.

Book of Parables The Final Judgement of Amaze and the Watchers and their children are discussed in this section, which also gives the names and functions of the Fallen Angels.

Book of the Heavenly Luminaires This is concerned with astronomy.

Dream Visions The Fall of the Angels and their punishment by the Archangels is described here.

Epistle of Enoch Here is the foretelling of the terrors of the Day of Judgement and the punishment of sinners.

Third Book of Enoch also called the "Hebrew Apocalypse of Enoch" as it survives in Hebrew.

It is thought that the earliest of the three *Books of Enoch*, which are not included in the *Bible*, was written by different authors some time around the 3rd century BCE. Fragments from the *First Book of Enoch* have also been discovered in Qumran among the *Dead Sea Scrolls* and are thought to have

The Angelic Hierarchy

While followers of most of the world's religions believe in Angels, this is actually a generic term for a wide range of celestial beings of various "ranks," including those at the lowest level closest to us on Earth.

In the *Old Testament* there are the Malach, Irinim, Cherubim, Sarim, Seraphim, and Ofanim. In the *New Testament* St Paul writes of Principalities, Thrones, Dominations, Virtues, and Powers. Today, the most widely accepted theory about the rank of Angelic beings is that detailed by Pseudo-Dionysius the Areopagite, thought to have been written some time between 485 and 518–28 CE. The surviving writings in Latin, *On the celestial* hierarchy (*De ecclesiastica hierarchia*), describe the now commonly used division of three Hierarchies, Spheres, or Triads of Angels, with each Hierarchy containing three Orders, or Choirs. In descending order of power his ranking of the Angelic Hierarchy is:

First Hierarchy

The Angels of the First Hierarchy are the closest to God and are of equal rank to each other.

Three Hierarchies

In descending order of power the ranking of the Angelic Hierarchy is:

First Hierarchy	Second Hierarchy	Third Hierarchy
Seraphim	Dominions	Principalities
Cherubim	Virtues	Archangels
Thrones or Ofanim	Powers	Angels

Seraphim (singular "Seraph") is the highest order of Angels. They are the caretakers of God's throne and encircle it continuously, singing His praises: 'Holy, holy, holy is the Lord of Hosts. All the Earth is filled with His glory'. It is said that they radiate an intense blinding light so that nothing, not even the other Angelic orders, can look upon them. In *Isaiah 6:2* we have a full description of how the Seraphim appear, with their four faces and six wings.

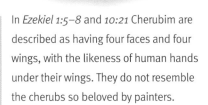

Choir of Angels

Cherubim (singular "Cherub") hold the knowledge of God and are often sent to Earth to perform God's tasks. They are the guardians of light and of the Moon and stars. They are also the record keepers of Heaven. Cherubim are the first Angels to be mentioned in the *Bible* when two Cherubim are placed by God to guard the gates to Eden with a flaming sword:

> *He drove out man; and he placed at the east of the garden of Eden Cherubims, and a flaming sword which turned every way, to keep the way of the tree of life.*
> GENESIS 3:24, KING JAMES BIBLE

In *Ezekiel 1:5–8* and *10:21* Cherubim are described as having four faces and four wings, with the likeness of human hands under their wings. They do not resemble the cherubs so beloved by painters.

Thrones, or Ofanim, are also known as "Wheels" and "the many-eyed Ones," as in the Prophet Ezekiel's visions of the Throne of God (Merkavah). In *Ezekiel 1* they are described as having the appearance of wheels within wheels, with their rims covered with eyes. They are the dispensers of God's judgment, acting with impartiality.

Second Hierarchy

The Angels of the Second Hierarchy act as Heavenly counselors.

Dominions, Dominations, or Hashmallim, oversee the lower Angelic realms. They receive their orders from the Seraphim, Cherubim, or God Himself. They are responsible for keeping the Cosmos in order and rarely make themselves known to humankind. They have been described as wearing long gowns reaching to their feet hitched with a golden belt. They carry emblems of their authority: a golden staff with their right hand and the Seal of God in the left. At other times they are said to hold an orb or a scepter.

Virtues, Fortresses, or Strongholds, lie beyond the Thrones and are equal to the Principalities. They maintain the aspects of the material world, overseeing groups of people. These are the Angels who make miracles occur. Those who are able to raise

Two
Dominion
Angels

their spiritual consciousness often connect with the Virtues. They are said to be shaped like sparks of light, and they inspire humankind in artistic, musical, and scientific endeavors.

Powers are the Angels of birth and death who guard the boundaries between Heaven and Earth, making sure that the souls who leave the mortal world transcend to Heaven safely. They are the bearers of conscience and the keepers of the history of humankind known as the Akashic records. They oversee the distribution of power among humankind and can influence philosophy, theology, religion, and ideology. It is the duty of the

Savoaph, God the Father, *Victor Mikhailovich Vasnetsov, 1885–96, oil on canvas, Tretgakov Gallery, Moscow, Russia.*

Powers to protect the world from the infiltration of demons and to protect our souls from their power. They are said to be shaped like brightly colored hazy fumes.

Angels in each Hierarchy

The Seraphim include:
Barakiel (or Babiel), Seraphiel,
Metatron, Michael, Uriel, Nathanael,
Jehoel, Chamuel, Samael, and
Lucifer, before he fell from Grace.

The Cherubim include:
Gabriel, Raphael, Uriel, Zophiel,
Cherubiel, Ophaniel, and Azazel.

The Thrones include:
Bodiel, Jophiel, Oriphiel, Tzaphkiel,
Raziel, and Samael.

The Dominions include:
Hashmal, Zadkiel, Muriel,
and Zacharael (Yahriel).

The Virtues include:
Chamuel, Uriel, Gabriel, Michael,
Tarshish, Peliel, Barbiel, Sabriel,
Haniel, and Hamaliel.

The Powers include:
Gabriel, Raphael, Camael,
and Verchiel.

The Principalities include:
Anael, Haniel, Cerviel, Amael,
Nisroc, and Requel.

The Archangels include:
Gabriel, Raphael, Michael, Metatron,
Uriel, Chamuel, Zadkiel, Jophiel,
Haniel, Sandalphon, Raziel, Raguel,
Jeremiel, and Satan (before his fall).

Third Hierarchy

The Angels of the Third Hierarchy act as
Heavenly messengers.

Principalities are the Angels who watch
over the mortal world and are considered
to be the guardians of the Earth's nations,
cities, towns, and sacred sites. Concerned
with the events and issues involving these,
including politics and the world's leaders,
trade, and commerce, they are also charged
with managing the duties of the Angels. The
Principalities are shaped like rays of light.

Archangels (see page 38) are the
messengers of God and act as the
administrative leaders of all the Angelic
orders. There are millions of Archangels who
watch over the entire Universe, but certain
Archangels have been specifically chosen
to look after humanity. The Archangels are
known to work on several different levels—
they often belong to the other Choirs or
orders, such as Cherubim and Seraphim,
yet they enjoy working with humans when
called upon to do so.

The confusion about the groupings of the
celestial rank of Archangels arises from the
ancient way of defining Angels, which was
simply Angel and Archangel. It was not until

later that the Hierarchy was defined and many of the Angels previously just referred to as Archangels were listed as members of different levels of the Hierarchy. The number of Archangels has long been a source of great discussion. Traditionally there are seven, although who they are and what they do seems to vary according to different sources.

Angels are the most familiar order known to people. They watch over individual souls, guiding and protecting them. There are millions of different types of Angels who not only bring joy and love into our lives, but also help guide us through every part of our existence on this planet. We mainly aspire to communicate with the Angels who are charged with looking after our own personal existence. Angels are mentioned regularly throughout the *Old* and *New Testament*, but they are often not individually named.

Principality Angels watch over the Cosmos

Angels & the Seven Heavens

Many see the spiritual Universe in which we live as made up of Seven Heavens with the Earth beneath. This belief, with its roots in ancient Sumerian texts, is an integral part of Christianity, Islam, and Judaism. In Jewish mysticism, the Seven Heavens are seen as levels of the Divine consciousness governed by Angels.

With the help of Angels and spiritual guides, you can move through levels of spiritual consciousness represented by the Heavens.

The First Heaven Vilon (Latin *Velum, meaning curtain*), also called Shamayim or Shamajim. This is the closest Heavenly realm to the Earth. Governed by the Archangel Gabriel, it is described in the *Talmud* as being "rolled up and down to enable the Sun to go in and out." Vilon is home to the astronomer Angels

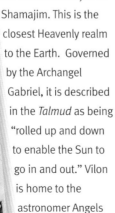

who preside over the stars, and to the Angels who control the elements such as the weather and water.

The Second Heaven Raqia, also called Rakia (meaning expanse). This is ruled over by the Archangels Zachariel and Raphael. It is where the Fallen Angels are held prisoner, awaiting the Final Judgment, and where sinners await the Day of Judgment.

The Third Heaven Shechakim also called Shehaqim (meaning skies). This is the domain of the Angel Anahel and three subordinate sarim (Hebrew for "princes"), an order of singing Angels. The *Second Book of Enoch* states that both Paradise and Hell are contained within Shechakim. Paradise is situated in the southern half, with the souls entering through golden gates (the biblical "pearly gates"); Hell is "on the northern side."

The Fourth Heaven Zevul, also known as Zebhul (the "lofty place," *Isaiah 63:15*). This realm is ruled over by the Archangel Michael. It is here that Jerusalem and the Holy Temple exist in the spiritual realm.

The Fifth Heaven Ma'on (the "residence" or "dwelling"). This is governed by the Archangel Sandalphon. Here God's praises are sung during the night by choirs of Angels.

The Sixth Heaven Machon (the "habitation" or "resting place," *Deuteronomy 26:15*). The realm of Zachiel, this is a stormy, snowy Heaven located behind doors of fire. The Akashic records of the Earth's history, and every being who ever lived, are stored here.

The Seventh Heaven Aravot, also called Araboth or Arabot (the "clouds," *Psalms 68:5*). The highest Heaven, under Cassie, houses the Throne of Glory, attended by the Archangels, where God dwells. Underneath the Throne lie all unborn human souls.

Aravot, the Seventh Heaven

Ma'on, the Fifth Heaven

Machon, the Sixth Heaven

Shechakim, the Third Heaven

Zevul, the Fourth Heaven

Vilon, the First Heaven

Raqia, the Second Heaven

Fallen Angels

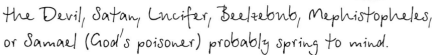

When we think of the dark forces that encourage us to do wrong, we normally think back to stories about Fallen Angels that most of us have heard since childhood. Names such as the Devil, Satan, Lucifer, Beelzebub, Mephistopheles, or Samael (God's poisoner) probably spring to mind.

To many Jews and Christians a Fallen Angel is one that has been banished from Heaven for disobeying or rebelling against God, and there are a number of beliefs and stories regarding why Fallen Angels were cast out.

Lust

In the "Book of Watchers," which is part of the *First Book of Enoch* (see page 24), the following legend demonstrates how lust caused the Fall of the Angels from Heaven:

God asked the "Watchers" (also called Grigori), a select group of Angels, to help the Archangels in the creation of the Garden of Eden. The Grigori who descended to Earth saw the beautiful daughters of man and lusted after them. Two hundred Angels, under the leadership of twenty captains, descended to the summit of Mount Hermon, planning to choose wives for themselves and have children with them. Their leader, Shemhazai, warned them that this would be a great sin—he feared that they would not go through with the plan and he alone would pay the penalty—so they agreed to swear an oath binding themselves together and committing to the plan. The issue from these mixed marriages was a race of giants called the Nephilim or Anakim/Anak (Giants) who consumed everything that humankind had to offer. When there was nothing left the giants started to devour humankind, then they began to sin against birds, beasts, reptiles, and fish. Finally they fought and started to kill each other.

The book also describes how the Fallen Angels—mainly Azazael—teach humans how to make swords, knives, shields, and breastplates. Azazael also reveals to humans the metals in the Earth, and teaches how to work them into jewelry and trinkets. He also tells humans about cosmetics. Shemhazai teaches spell-making, Barakel astrology, Kawkabel astronomy, Ezekeel augury from the clouds, Arakiel the signs of the Earth, Samsaweel the signs of the Sun, and Seriel the signs of the Moon.

Punishment

The Archangels Michael, Uriel, Raphael, and Gabriel appealed to God to judge the inhabitants of the world and the Fallen Angels. Uriel is sent by God to tell Noah of the coming apocalypse, giving him instructions to build the Ark so that "he may escape and his seed may be preserved for all the generations of the world." God then sends the Great Flood to cleanse the Earth of the wanton killing and destruction caused by

the Nephilim, and to destroy each and every one of them. God commands the Archangel Raphael to imprison Azazael in the darkness, so that he may never see light again; on the Day of Judgment he will be cast into the fire. The remaining Fallen Angels are confined forever in a prison of torment and fire.

Judgment, a Tarot card by Oliver Burston.

Pride

Lucifer's rebellion against God involves Pride, the gravest of the seven deadly sins, and his story is well known among Christians. He was the first and mightiest Angel to be created, second only to God himself and much loved by Him. With his power unmatched by any other Angel in Heaven, Lucifer became ambitious and self-centered and decided to prove his power by raising his throne to the same height as God's. This rebellion caused him to be thrown out of Heaven into the abyss. A third of the Angel host defected from the light with him, becoming Dark Angels who tempt humankind into evil, lustful ways.

Bowing to Humankind

There is another belief that after God created humans, he wanted His Angels to acknowledge them by bowing down before them, but some Angels would not obey. Those who refused were cast out of Heaven.

Good and Evil: The Devil Tempting a Young Woman, *André J. V. Orsel, 1832, oil on canvas, Musée des Beaux Arts, Lyon, France. Peter Willi/The Bridgeman Art Library.*

Temptation to Sin

I firmly believe that the powerful a who try to sway us to the "dark side" are emissaries of God, sent to test our strength of will. When we are incarnated on this planet we all have free choice in the way we want to live our lives. Without the presence of evil we would always be in a state of purity and goodness. There would be no learning new lessons in our present incarnate without the choices placed before us that test our dark side. In *Isaiah 45:7* God states, "I form the light and create darkness. I make peace and create evil." This demonstrates that He is actually in control of the Fallen Angels and they are part of His higher plans for us.

The Archangel Lucifer volunteered to oversee the Angelic forces to try to tempt us from the path of goodness. He and his followers agreed to be separated from the occupants of Heaven and to use their vast power to tempt us into evil ways. However, once this grand experiment is completed, we are told that Lucifer and his minions will be returned to their rightful place in Heaven.

The Archangels

There are millions of Archangels in the Cosmos, but only a few are known by name and connect with us on Earth. The names of all the Archangels that we are familiar with end with the "el" suffix apart from two —Metatron and Sandalphon—considered to be the only Archangels in Heaven who were originally mortal.

Archangels can be in many different places simultaneously without restrictions of space and time. They are often the bearers of messages. Although a fundamental part of Jewish, Christian, and Muslim beliefs, Archangels are nondenominational, so they will connect with and help anyone, regardless of their beliefs.

References to Archangels are found in many different places, including the *Bible*, the three *Books of Enoch*, the *Koran,* and the *Lists of Dionysius*. The main Judeo-Christian Archangels are often named as Michael, Raphael, Gabriel, Uriel, Chamuel, Jophiel, and Raguel. Traditional Kabbalah adds Metatron, Raziel, Zadkiel, Chamuel (known as Khamael by Kabbalists), and Sandalphon to this list.

Uriel and Ariel appear on some lists as one Angel although other sources suggest that they are two different beings. Islam recognizes four Archangels—Gabriel (Djibril, Jibrail, Jibril or Jibraaiy), Michael (Mikail, Mika'il or Mikaaiyl), Raphael (Israfil or Israafiyl), and Azrael.

Many people have reached a stage in their spiritual development in which they are communicating, or attempting to communicate, with the Archangels. In this chapter I have referred to the Archangels whose skills and energies are most evident at this present time. Remember, when you are calling upon your Archangels to be with you, it often happens that you will become aware instantly of their Angelic presence.

Emblems of Saints Matthew and Mark, *Philip Webb, 1863, drawing on paper, Tate, London, UK.*

Ariel

The Archangel Ariel, whose name means "Lion of God," is known as the Archangel of the Earth as he watches over the natural world.

Together with the Archangel Raphael, Ariel is involved with protecting and healing the natural world—the environment and wildlife. Ariel can help us to understand the balance of the natural world and how we can help to preserve it.

Spiritual Associations

Ariel will help you to appreciate and have reverence for all life forms and can help you to understand the realities that surround you.

Azrael

The Archangel Azrael, whose name means "Whom God Helps," is also given the unpleasant title "Angel of Death."

Azrael's principal role is to help people cross over to Heaven at the time of their physical death. He gives comfort to people prior to their physical death, and he helps them to assimilate on the other side. He will also work with those left grieving on this planet by surrounding them with healing and loving energy. Azrael is described as having four faces and 4,000 wings, with his body consisting of eyes and tongues—the number of which corresponds to the number of people on Earth. It is said that every time he blinks his eyes it is a sign that another person has died. He records the births of the living and erases the names of those who have died in a large book. Azrael is also known as Izra'il or Ezra'il and is one of the four Archangels of Islam.

Spiritual Associations

Call upon Azrael to comfort and support you in times of grief following a bereavement. You can also call out to him to help people you know who are in need of his love and healing energies at such times.

Love and the Pilgrim, *Sir Edward Burne-Jones, 1896–97, oil painting, Tate, London, UK.*

Gabriel

The Archangel Gabriel, whose name means "God is my Strength," is known as the "messenger Angel" and is important in Judeo-Christian and Islamic religious lore. He is one of only two Angels mentioned by name in the Old Testament—the other being the Archangel Michael.

In the *Old Testament* it is said that Gabriel was the Angel who destroyed Sodom on the orders of God and who parted the waters of the Red Sea when the Israelites were fleeing Egypt under the leadership of Moses. In the *New Testament*, he appeared to both Mary and her cousin Elizabeth to announce the future births of their sons Jesus and John the Baptist. In Islam, Gabriel translates into Jibril and it is Jibril who revealed the *Koran* to the Prophet Mohammed.

Gabriel is a powerful Archangel. Those who need to make an important decision, such as a career change or a house move, should call upon him for wisdom and confidence. As well as a direct messenger of the Divine, he is also charged with looking after the purity of the water on Earth and the fertility of all life forms.

The Annunciation, *Fra Angelico, c. 1430–32, tempera and gold on panel, Prado, Madrid, Spain.*

Spiritual Associations

As well as guiding decisions about your future, Gabriel can assist you in interpreting your dreams, and help you feel his energies of inspiration, motivation, and wisdom. If you feel that your spiritual vision and energies are blocked, call upon Gabriel to clear your third eye and to remove any other blockages that are hindering you. Also call upon him if you feel your body is full of toxins and needs purifying or if your thoughts are negative, or even destructive, and they need clearing

Chamuel

The Archangel Chamuel, whose name means "He who sees God" or "He who seeks God," is the Archangel of pure love who can help lift you from the depths of sorrow to find healing in your heart.

He is also in charge of world peace, and is known by a number of other names, including Camael, Camiel, Camiul, Camniel, Cancel, Jahoel, Kemuel, Khamael, and Seraphiel. Chamuel can help you to build new relationships, both platonic and romantic, on strong and lasting foundations. He can also help you to express love through creative talents such as writing and painting. If your heart is broken or bruised, call upon the Archangel Chamuel to help you heal. If your heart is full of negative emotions, or is blocked by unforgiving emotions, ask the Archangel Chamuel to help you feel forgiveness. He can also help to repair misunderstandings in both personal and work relationships.

Spiritual Associations

Chamuel can help you to attract soulmates, and he can teach you to overcome negative feelings toward yourself and others.

Haniel

The Archangel Haniel, whose name means the "Grace of God" or the "Glory of God," is generally credited with the title of Chief or Prince of the Orders of Principalities and Virtues.

In some Kabbalist texts he is known for escorting Enoch to the spiritual realms, where he was transformed into an Angel. Haniel can help us to rediscover the lost secrets of natural healing remedies such as crystals, herbs, powders, and potions. This Archangel can also assist understanding of how to harness the power of the Moon, and how to relate to its healing energies. Haniel can also be called upon to help those who need poise and confidence before an event such as speaking in public, being interviewed for a new job, or even going on a first date.

Spiritual Associations

Haniel can help bring inspiration, harmony, common sense, and loving friends into your life. If you feel weak and unsure, call upon the Archangel Haniel to give you the strength and determination. He can help you develop your communication and channeling abilities, linking you with the Cosmos.

Jeremiel

The Archangel Jeremiel, whose name means "Mercy of God," is the overseer of souls who are waiting to reincarnate.

Once we have crossed over, Jeremiel, also known as Ramiel, helps us to look back over our lives on Earth. While we are still here, he can help us review our present lives through psychic dreams, visions, and clairvoyance so that we make positive life changes.

Spiritual Associations

Archangel Jeremiel will help you to view your life with clarity and assist you with positive life changes, as well as with the development of your clairvoyant and intuitive abilities in both your waking and dream life. He can help to motivate you if you feel at a crossroads in your spiritual growth and need to find a sense of personal direction.

An Angel Piping to the Souls in Hell, *Evelyn De Morgan, 19th century, oil painting.*

Jophiel

The Archangel Jophiel, whose name means "Beauty of God," is the Archangel of art and beauty and is the Patron Archangel of artists. He is also known as Iofiel, Iophiel, Jofiel, and Zophiel.

He can inspire us to create beautiful images, have positive thoughts, and see the beauty in all things, including people. He is also the Archangel through whom all information, perception, knowledge, and ideas flow. He can assist us in discovering hidden strengths and abilities within ourselves. The Archangel Jophiel is also involved in helping to cleanse the Earth of pollution and safeguard it against damage, in order to preserve its beauty for the enjoyment of future generations of humankind. He can also help you to overcome inertia and feelings of depression and low self-esteem.

Spiritual Associations

Jophiel can encourage a deeper understanding of who you are and your life's purpose. By helping you to strengthen the connection with your Higher Self, he can promote your communication with your spiritual guides and Angels.

Metatron

The Archangel Metatron is one of the two Archangels whose name does not end in the letters "el." The meaning of the name "Metatron" is unclear, but suggested meanings include "he who occupies the throne next to the Divine throne" or "the Angel of the Presence" and many consider him the greatest and most powerful of all the Angels.

It is said that Metatron once lived upon this Earth as the Prophet and scribe Enoch, who was also a scholar of the Heavenly secrets. He was taken by God directly to the Seventh Heaven—the highest level—to reside and work. Here God transformed him into an Archangel. In appearance, he is said to have 36 pairs of wings. Metatron is mentioned in the Kabbalah and is reputed to have been the Angel who led the Hebrew tribes through the wilderness to safety after the Exodus. In the *New Testament* he is said to have been the light that St Paul encountered on the road to Damascus.

In Heaven, Metatron organizes and oversees the keepers of the Akashic records, which are the history, memories, and thoughts of humankind. He is charged with filtering the pure energy of the Cosmos into a vibration that can be used without the destruction of the physical form. He is the Patron Archangel of children, overseeing their safety and education on Earth as well as helping those children who cross over to Heaven to adjust.

Spiritual Associations

Metatron helps us to grow spiritually so that we can learn to communicate with the Angelic Realms. He can encourage you to find inner peace and tranquility by assisting you in balancing your emotions.

Michael

The Archangel Michael, whose name is a question "Who is like God?," was the first Angel created by God and is the leader of the Archangels. He leads the Heavenly forces in the fight against the legions of the Angels of Darkness.

In the *Old Testament*, he rescued Daniel and his friends from the lion's den and in the *New Testament* he forewarned Mary of her approaching death. He is often visualized as wearing a cobalt blue cloak and carrying a sword of either metal or living flame. This sword can be used to cut through the cords that bind us to the past and negative emotions, and can protect us from the dark forces that seek to lead us astray.

Michael is the Patron Archangel of police officers and it is he you should call if you feel afraid for your own personal safety. He is the Angel of protection, justice, and strength, and can give you guidance on making changes.

Spiritual Associations

Call upon Michael for courage and strength in mind and body, helping you to banish fear, low self-esteem and a lack of commitment or motivation. Michael can give you guidance as to your life's purpose and how to achieve it, and can protect you from psychic attack. He gives protection to those "lightworkers" who are already open to the spiritual realms.

Michael

Raguel

The Archangel Raguel, whose name means "Friend of God," is the Archangel of fairness, justice, and harmony, and the champion of underdogs. Call upon him if you feel you are being manipulated, treated unfairly, or being overpowered by others.

He will give you wisdom, understanding, and direction as to how to break free from this pattern, and how to attain balanced power and fairness. He is one of the seven Archangels listed in the *Books of Enoch* and is the Angel who elevated Enoch up to Heaven. Raguel keeps all the other Archangels and Angels in order, making sure that they are working harmoniously with humankind and with each other. His actions have sometimes been misconstrued as being against his fellow Angels, leading people to misinterpret his role and consider him a demon. However, he is merely keeping order within the Angelic ranks, and making sure that there is no corruption or wrongdoing. It is said that on the Day of Judgment he will call forth the other Angels to deal with the unpure.

Spiritual Associations

Raguel can help you to achieve harmony and balance in your life, and find the wisdom to act fairly and with justice when faced with conflict or bullying behavior.

Raphael

The Archangel Raphael, whose name means "God has Healed," is a powerful healer, on both a personal and a planetary level, and is charged with maintaining the atmosphere of the planet.

Raphael, also known as Labbiel, is said to be the chief of the Guardian Angels. He is also known as the Patron Archangel of those who practise in the medical field. Legend has it that Raphael gave the *Book of Science and Knowledge* to Noah to help him rebuild the Earth after the Great Flood. Raphael is one of the most frequently painted Angels in western art, depicted by Botticelli, Titian, and Rembrandt.

Spiritual Associations

Raphael can help with the healing of mind, body, and spirit, assisting you not only with physical but with emotional pain. He can encourage you to develop your ability for creative visualization and enhance your intuitive and clairvoyant capabilities. Raphael can even teach you the mysteries of the Cosmos, translating them into conscious thought if you enlist his help.

Raphael

Raziel

The Archangel Raziel, whose name means "the Secret of God," is believed to know all of the secrets and functions of the Universe and works very closely with God.

He is said to have recorded these secrets in *The Book of the Angel Raziel*, which was given to Adam for guidance after he and Eve were expelled from the Garden of Eden. Raziel also gave a copy to Enoch, prior to his ascension and transformation into the Archangel Metatron. The Archangel Raphael is said to have given a copy of this work to Noah, who used the information inside to build his ark and to help humankind after the Great Flood. Raziel is the Patron Archangel of law makers and lawyers.

Spiritual Associations

Raziel can help you to comprehend esoteric knowledge. He can also assist you in developing your psychic gifts to the optimum, including your abilities in telepathy, intuition, clairvoyance, clairaudience, and clairsentience. Raziel can promote your self-awareness and guide you in your search for knowledge—both spiritual and factual, in relation to the physical world.

Sandalphon

The Archangel Sandalphon does not have a traditional meaning for his name, although he is often called "Prince of Prayers."

One of the two Archangels whose name does not end with an "el," Sandalphon is the Archangel Metatron's twin brother and was formerly the human prophet Elijah. Elijah, as a reward for his good work as a mortal man, was lifted into Heaven in a fiery chariot pulled by two fiery horses carried in a whirlwind (*Second Book of Kings 2:11*), where he was transformed into the Angel Sandalphon. He is said to be the tallest Angel, extending from the Earth to Heaven. Sandalphon's main role is to carry the prayers of humankind to God, and he also protects unborn children. Kabbalists believe that he can help expectant parents determine the gender of their unborn child. Guardian of the Earth, he is responsible for the wellbeing of its inhabitants.

Spiritual Associations

Sandalphon can help you understand and use the spiritual gifts of healing and distant healing, while making sure that you are "grounded" and thereby protecting you.

Tzaphkiel

The Archangel Tzaphkiel, whose name means "The Scribe of the Divine," is charged with bringing the Divine laws into physical manifestation and expression.

For those who are deserving, he will reveal the answers to all their questions and allow them to glimpse the knowledge contained in the Akashic records. Tzaphkiel is often called upon to bring an unwanted situation to an end, or to bring a swift closure to long-term pain. He is closely associated with death and is often perceived as the Archangel of death. However, he is also the Archangel of life because, without an ending, there cannot be a new beginning, which gives you the opportunity for transformation.

Spiritual Associations

Tzaphkiel can assist with spiritual growth by helping you to gain wisdom and understanding. He can help you reach a higher altered state of consciousness, through enhancing and accelerating your meditative abilities. This leads to spiritual progress through increasing your connection with the Angelic realms.

Uriel

The Archangel Uriel, whose name means "Fire of God," is known as the Archangel of enlightenment, insight, and physical order. He is said to be one of the wisest of the Archangels and you should call upon him if you have a problem you need to solve.

You may not realize that he has answered your prayer or question until you unexpectedly and suddenly come up with a brilliant or "off the wall" solution. Uriel is also associated with spiritual understanding and studies, and works very closely with the Earth and Earth healing. He is in charge of the weather and with helping the planet to recover from natural disasters, such as earthquakes, floods, hurricanes, tornadoes, and fires. It is said that God sent Uriel to forewarn Noah of the Great Flood and that he gave Adam a book of medicinal herbs and humankind the knowledge of alchemy, Kabbalah, and prophetic visions. He is also considered to be the Patron Archangel of writers.

Spiritual Associations

Uriel can bring spirituality into your everyday life. He can help you make your way in the material world, and enable you to have the clarity and insight to understand the hidden agendas of others.

Uriel

The Sacrifice of Isaac, *Domenichino (Domenico Zampieri), 1641, oil on canvas, Prado, Madrid, Spain.*

Zadkiel

The Archangel Zadkiel, whose name means "Righteousness of God," is the Angel of mercy and compassion and also one of the Angels of charity.

He is said to be the chief of the Order of Dominions and one of the seven Archangels who stand before the throne of God. Zadkiel is also thought to be the Angel who stayed the hand of Abraham from sacrificing his son Isaac as an offering to God. He can help soothe and comfort us when we are going through times of despair and sorrow.

Spiritual Associations

Zadkiel can help you clear your mind and aspire to higher levels of consciousness, especially when meditating, unblocking your mind by clearing emotional debris. He can help you feel kindness and forgiveness toward yourself and others and help you to scrutinize others with compassion instead of judgment.

Jewish prayer at bedtime to the Archangels

There is a traditional prayer to be said before bedtime called "the Bedtime Shema" (Kriat Sh'ma), which can still be found in more traditional prayer books today. The recital of the Shema before retiring is considered to act as a protection against the dangers of the night. The following section of the Shema invokes the four Archangels Michael, Gabriel, Uriel, and Raphael. The prayer ends invoking the Shekhinah, which is the feminine presence of God—often visualized as a woman with white wings who hovers over the bed like a canopy of protection.

*In the name of Adonai, God of Israel
May the Angel Michael be at my right,
The Angel Gabriel at my left,
And before me the Angel Uriel,
And the Angel Raphael behind me
And above my head
The Shekinah (Divine Presence).*

Angel Meditation

This can be done as a structured meditative exercise as described, or it is also wonderful to do it in bed before you go to sleep. Remember, if you do not sleep straightaway, you must close yourself down as described.

1 *Take yourself to a quiet place where you will not be disturbed, or perhaps to your sacred space (see page 80). Remove your shoes and place your feet flat on the floor.*

2 *Close your eyes and concentrate on your breathing. I always suggest breathing in for the count of four through your nose and exhaling for the count of four through your mouth.*

Be aware of the soles of your feet on the floor and visualize them anchored there by strong roots growing from them, which are penetrating deep into the ground with each in-breath until you feel securely fastened.

Now, as you inhale, visualize the white light of the Universe entering your body, filling it up.

As you exhale, feel stress and negative energies flow out of you. Be aware of your body and feel it relaxing.

3 *When you are ready, mentally invoke the Archangel Michael to grant you his presence on your right side. Let yourself feel his energy; it could be a slight tingling, pressure, breeze, heat, or some other sensation. If you cannot*

feel anything, visualize his reassuring presence standing next to you.

4 *The Archangel Michael is the Angel of protection. Inwardly ask him to let you feel his strength and to give protection to you and others who may be in need of it.*

Taking your time, and concentrating inwardly, ask the Archangel Michael if he has a message for you.

When you are ready to move on, thank him for his presence and then invoke the Archangel Gabriel to make his presence felt on your left side.

5 *As before, try to feel the energy of the Angel Gabriel's strength on your left side, together with the protection of the Archangel Michael on your right side.*

Ask the Archangel Gabriel to give you insight so that you may always be with God. Ask him to remove all your fears and negative thoughts.

Again pause and ask Gabriel if he has any message for you. When you are ready to move on, thank him for his presence.

6 *Now invoke the Archangel Uriel to grant you his presence in front of you. As he is the Archangel of enlightenment and wisdom ask him for his guidance.*

If you have a problem that needs solving, ask him to help you. Be alert for any wisdom or advice that he may have for you. Feel now that you are surrounded by the three energies: protection, strength, and wisdom.

Ask the Archangel Uriel if he has any message for you; when you are ready, thank him and move on.

7 Next invoke the Archangel Raphael to visit you with his healing energy. Try to sense him behind you. If you, or others you know, need his healing attributes ask him inwardly to help you or them.

Feel the different energies of the four Archangels now surrounding you with their individual powers—protection, strength, wisdom, and healing. Thank the Archangel Raphael for his presence.

8 When you are ready, ask the Archangels for their love, help, guidance, and protection for you, your loved ones, your friends, and then for the whole planet. You may feel their response in a number of ways. Enjoy the blanket of love, serenity, and peace from your Angels surrounding you.

Bathe in the wonderful feeling of being surrounded by these four powerful Archangels. Feel secure as their harmonious energies envelope you, letting you feel at peace with yourself.

9 When you feel that you would like to finish, thank all of your Angels again in turn— starting with Raphael, then Uriel, then Gabriel, and finally Michael—for their presence and feel each one of them leaving you.

10 Become aware of your breathing again and visualize the roots that grew from the soles of your feet returning back to their source. Become aware of your body; when you feel ready, move a little on your chair, perhaps stretching a little. Take your time before standing up.

ANGELS OF THE SEASONS

The seasons, elements, and directions each have an
Archangel who is responsible for them as follows:

Season	Archangel	Element	Direction
Spring	Raphael	Air	East
Summer	Michael	Fire	South
Autumn	Gabriel	Water	West
Winter	Uriel	Earth	North

GOVERNING ANGELS OF THE DAYS OF THE WEEK

Every day of the week and every hour of the day has its own governing Angel.
Working with the Angel who is presiding over a particular day, or perhaps a specific
hour of a particular day, is a very powerful way to be in contact with Angels.

Day of Week	Archangel	Angel
Sunday	Raphael	Michael
Monday	Gabriel	Gabriel
Tuesday	Khamael	Zamael
Wednesday	Michael	Raphael
Thursday	Zadkiel	Sachiel
Friday	Haniel	Anael
Saturday	Tzaphkiel	Cassiel

GOVERNING ANGELS OF THE HOURS OF THE DAY

Hour	Sunday	Monday	Tuesday	Wednesday	Thursday	Friday	Saturday
1am	Michael	Gabriel	Samael	Raphael	Sachiel	Anael	Cassiel
2am	Anael	Cassiel	Michael	Gabriel	Samael	Raphael	Sachiel
3am	Raphael	Sachiel	Anael	Cassiel	Michael	Gabriel	Samael
4am	Gabriel	Samael	Raphael	Sachiel	Anael	Cassiel	Michael
5am	Cassiel	Michael	Gabriel	Samael	Raphael	Sachiel	Anael
6am	Sachiel	Anael	Cassiel	Michael	Gabriel	Samael	Raphael
7am	Samael	Raphael	Sachiel	Anael	Cassiel	Michael	Gabriel
8am	Michael	Gabriel	Samael	Raphael	Sachiel	Anael	Cassiel
9am	Anael	Cassiel	Michael	Gabriel	Samael	Raphael	Sachiel
10am	Raphael	Sachiel	Anael	Cassiel	Michael	Gabriel	Samael
11am	Gabriel	Samael	Raphael	Sachael	Anael	Cassiel	Michael
12pm	Cassiel	Michael	Gabriel	Samael	Raphael	Sachiel	Anael
1pm	Sachael	Anael	Cassiel	Michael	Gabriel	Samael	Raphael
2pm	Samael	Raphael	Sachiel	Anael	Cassiel	Michael	Gabriel
3pm	Michael	Gabriel	Samael	Raphael	Sachiel	Anael	Cassiel
4pm	Anael	Cassiel	Michael	Gabriel	Samael	Raphael	Sachiel
5pm	Raphael	Sachiel	Anael	Cassiel	Michael	Gabriel	Samael
6pm	Gabriel	Samael	Raphael	Sachiel	Anael	Cassiel	Michael
7pm	Cassiel	Michael	Gabriel	Samael	Raphael	Sachiel	Anael
8pm	Sachiel	Anael	Cassiel	Michael	Gabriel	Samael	Raphael
9pm	Samael	Raphael	Sachiel	Anael	Cassiel	Michael	Gabriel
10pm	Michael	Gabriel	Samael	Raphael	Sachiel	Anael	Cassiel
11pm	Anael	Cassiel	Michael	Gabriel	Samael	Raphael	Sachiel
12pm	Raphael	Sachiel	Anael	Cassiel	Michael	Gabriel	Samael

Guardian Angels

You never need to feel alone again; we all have a Guardian Angel who has been assigned to us by God and who is always with us protecting, guiding, comforting, and assisting us.

Your Guardian Angel has been with you from the time of your first incarnation and will be with you as you journey and evolve through each of your lifetimes. He is always by your side, giving you loving support, from the time of your birth on this planet through to the time of your Earthly death.

For every soul there is a Guardian watching over it.

KORAN 86:4

The lessons we are put onto this Earth to learn in each lifetime are already decided—many call this our Karma. Guardian Angels cannot interfere with our decisions because we have free will, but they will try to nudge and cajole us back onto the right path when we stray. However, our Guardian Angels cannot change our ultimate preordained destiny—which is why, tragically, children sometimes die so young. In these cases, most mystical and religious traditions agree that such souls came to Earth for a short time in order to learn a particular lesson.

A HELPING HAND

Although our Angels cannot help unless we make a pointed effort to invite them into our lives and make themselves known, they often try to commune with us or to help us in various ways—including through dreams, visions, and intuitive thoughts. There are times, however, when your Guardian Angel will connect with you without conscious invitation. This first contact often happens at times of great physical danger or even life-threatening situations. Your Guardian Angel will help you in a way that seems coincidental, so you may not realize at the time that you have received a helping hand.

I will never forget a time about 20 years ago, when I was in Israel and had taken my two eldest daughters to a museum. When we came out, we needed to find a taxi to take us back to the hotel. All along the front of the museum were lines of buses, so it was impossible to see the road to hail a taxi. As I stepped out from between two buses to find a taxi, I felt a strong energy pull me back. At the same time a bus whizzed past at top speed—if I had not been pulled back the bus would have killed me. Although I did not realize it at the time, my Guardian Angel had pulled me back, saving my life by a matter of seconds.

An Angel by your side

Michelle writes: Returning home from work at night, 18 years ago, I took the same route that I took every night from the station—along the main road to the alleyway that led to my street. I had taken this route for over a year in my boring life, and my boring job was just as usual—there was nothing different about the day. But the only way I can describe what happened next is that it felt like someone pulled their arms through me. It wasn't like being touched and pulled back by someone's hand—it was almost like a magnet was pulling at my core, pulling me back. It was as if someone strong had put their arms around my waist and was dragging me back—but without the sense of touch or pressure. I suddenly became very aware of a reluctance to go through the alleyway, so I turned back and walked around two blocks along the main road, entering my street from the opposite direction. I had never felt anything like that before and I also felt huge relief walking the long way around in clear sight of all the traffic—but also a bit stupid and embarrassed at being spooked by my own feelings. When I got home,

Guardian Angel, religious imagery for the Chinese market, *French school, 19th century, color litho, Bibliothèque Les Fontaines, Chantilly, France.*

I sat on my bed and thought about what had happened; I felt that if I told anyone I would sound like a mad person, so I kept it to myself.

The following night, as I returned from work and approached the alleyway I thought twice, but I felt perfectly safe so I walked through to my street and on home and went inside. My mom was in the kitchen with her friend Terry. They were both talking about a mugging/assault that had taken place in the alleyway the night before. "Oh my God!" I said and I told them about what had happened to me that night. They told me I had been very lucky—and of course mom started worrying about my journey home, offering to walk the dog to the station to meet me from work.

A few months later, a friend of mine arranged for us to see a medium or spiritualist . As soon as I sat down she explained that I was surrounded by lots of Guardian Angels, but then she said, 'But you already know that, that's why you did not walk through the alleyway that night.' I froze but I felt really excited too—looking back, it did feel like I was being pulled away for my own good. It also turns out that, along with my Guardian Angel, my aunt and my deceased grandparents are also watching over me.

Free Will

We all have the gift of free will, giving us freedom of choice over which pathways to follow in our life. Your Guardian Angel cannot stop you if you make the wrong decisions or align yourself with the "dark side" of your nature; but your Angel will try to prompt your conscience so you know the difference between right and wrong in all you do. When you begin to open up to connection with the Angelic realms, usually the first Angel who will converse with you is your Guardian Angel. One of their primary tasks is to help us to understand how to reconnect with our Creator through spiritual growth and knowledge. However, our Guardian Angels can do nothing for us unless we make an effort to ask them for help or guidance. When the answer comes, remember to thank your Guardian Angel for his assistance.

Life's Problems

Your Guardian Angel can bring you comfort during dark times and help you to see the light at the end of the tunnel. As our life progresses we go through many changes, mentally and physically. Our Guardian Angels help

us to overcome negative emotions, to embrace change and transform the ways we think and act.

If you find that you are having problems with another person—maybe a friend or even a co-worker—ask your Guardian Angel to have a word with their Guardian Angel. You may want this person to be nicer to you—or even leave you alone—and together the Guardian Angels may be able to help solve the problem. If you are having difficulties with a loved one you can try to reach out to their Guardian Angel directly to let them know how you feel. Often the Guardian Angels of others are willing to listen and will try to help—as long as their own charge is in no danger of being hurt in any way.

It is said that at the moment of conception the soul of the future child hovers above the couple. Alongside this soon-to-be-born soul is its Guardian Angel, who will be with the child throughout its life on Earth. Although some souls have asked to be reborn on Earth, some may still be a little frightened of what sufferings they will go through in what Kabbalists call this "Vale of

Tears." As our Guardian Angel demonstrates what lies ahead for the new soul on this planet, he will also give comfort by his reassurance that he will always be there no matter what.

As the world often seems in turmoil, with many dangers on our own doorsteps, it is important to try to establish a strong link with our Guardian Angels so that they can protect us from sources of negativity or evil around us. This can be done by frequently calling to your Guardian Angel to stand alongside you; invocations, meditations, and prayers can also help to strengthen this link.

Connecting with the Angelic realms through meditation

Connecting with your Guardian Angel

This meditation will help you to connect with your Guardian Angel. Each time you do it the connection should become stronger, as you open up the link between you. You may wish to have an exercise book or your Angelic journal (see page 84) with you to record the experience.

1 *Take yourself to a quiet place, sit comfortably, relax, remove your shoes, and place your feet on the floor; close your eyes. Become aware of your breathing. Breathe in through your nose for a count of four and exhale through your mouth for a count of four.*

2 *Invoke your Guardian Angel to grant you his attendance by your side. Sense his presence drawing closer and closer to you with each breath you take.*

3 *Now let your thoughts, or the questions you have for your Guardian Angel, form in your mind. Focus on the desire to hear the voice of your Guardian Angel. Listen for it with both your heart and mind. Be aware of any feelings that spring forth, as often our Guardian*

Angels first reach us in this way. Be open to any words or feelings that arise; contemplate them to see what they mean to you.

You may wish, at this point, to write down whatever you have received—which could be feelings, words, or pictures in your mind.

4 *When you are ready, thank your Angel and feel him take his leave. Concentrate on your breathing, open your eyes, and become aware of your surroundings.*

If you have time when you have finished this exercise, take a moment to read what you have written. You may be surprised at how the words affect you; you may feel touched and emotional. If you do, you can be sure that your Guardian Angel has connected with you.

An Angel is always there to provide guidance

YOUR GUARDIAN ANGEL'S NAME

It is a very human trait to give people and things names as this is our natural way to identify our world. Although our Angels do not need names, they are however very happy for you to call them by name. If you feel that you would like to call your Angel by a particular name, go ahead—he will not mind what you call him. Some people find they have a strong feeling about their Angel's name and if you feel this way, don't analyze it—go with the first name that comes to you. If you would like your Angel to give you his name, there are two ways in which you can ask for it.

Asking your Angel for a name

1 *Relax and either go through a meditative exercise, or just take some time out.*

2 *Become aware of your breathing; when you feel ready inwardly, call out to your Guardian Angel and ask him his name. The first name that pops into your head will be the answer.*

3 *Take a sheet of paper and write down your request. Before you go to sleep contemplate your written request, then put the sheet of paper under your pillow. Your Angel's name will come to you— either in a dream, or it will be etched on your mind when you wake up.*

EVERYDAY ANGELS

Angels, if invited, can play an important part in our everyday lives. These are Angels who have special skills relevant to all aspects of our lives, and who can offer help to ourselves and others.

Angels and Conception

If you are having trouble conceiving or maintaining a pregnancy, call upon the Archangel Gabriel. He is in charge of the fertility of all life forms on this planet, including humankind. Although I have written the following exercise as a short sitting meditation, my Angels tell me that it can also be done last thing at night when you are in bed.

The same exercise can also be done to invoke the Angel Lailah. The Angel Lailah can assist you because she is the guardian of human souls, watching over all the souls in Heaven. Once a soul has been chosen to descend to Earth, the Angel Lailah escorts it and plants it as a seed in the mother's womb. She tells the soul the secrets of the world and the languages of the animals. The Angel also reveals to the soul its history and its future. When the time comes for the child to be born she touches the baby's upper lip, creating an indention, to remind the baby to keep this knowledge secret.

Fertility meditation

1 *Take a moment and sit in a quiet place where you will not be disturbed, relax your body and concentrate on your breathing.*

2 *Invoke the Archangel Gabriel to come into your presence. Try to feel him next to you. You might find there is a tingle, a soft touch, or a sense of warmth. If you feel nothing, visualize him next to you.*

3 *Tell him what is making you unhappy. Ask him for his help. Take your time in his presence. Let him surround you with his energy and feel it enter your whole body. Breathe and relax.*

4 *When you are ready, thank him. Open your eyes, take your time, and rise up.*

Angel and baby

Choosing the Gender of a Child

Rabbinical lore tells us that the Archangel Sandalphon can help expectant parents determine the gender of their forthcoming child. If the gender is of particular importance to you invoke the Archangel Sandalphon to help you. The best way to do this is on the night of conception: Take a little time first to send out a plea to Sandalphon, asking him to help you become pregnant with the baby of whichever gender you require. It is very important that you state your reasons why the gender of the baby is so significant for you.

Childbirth

The Angel who protects the baby while it is in the womb is Armisael. In the *Talmud*, it is recommended that to ease a pregnancy *Psalm 20* should be recited nine times. If this is not effective, then one should invoke Armisael as follows:

I conjure you, Armisael, Angel who governs the womb, that you help this woman and the child in her body.

The Angel Temeluch (also called Temlakos or Temeluchus) is the protector of all children at their time of birth and in their early infancy. The Archangel Gabriel not only helps with conception but also with childbirth, guiding obstetricians in their work.

Children

It is normal to worry constantly about your children, but it can do more harm than good. Worry is a dark negative force, which can unintentionally affect those it is directed at. Our children are psychically linked to us and we should remain consciously aware of sending positive, loving, protective thoughts to them. Open up your mind and heart to their Guardian Angels and ask them to surround your children with rays of protection and love. By doing this you will bring your children's Guardian Angels that little bit closer to them.

Archangel of children

You can also invoke the Archangel Metatron who is the Patron Archangel of children to help:

1 *Find a quiet place where you will not be disturbed; sit down, relax and close your eyes.*

2 *Concentrate on your breathing and when you feel ready call upon the Archangel Metatron to help you.*

3 *Invoke him to send his protecting and loving energies to your child or children.*

Visualize them as you do this and see them in your mind's eye surrounded by a soft cloud, like a soap bubble, of whichever colour you want.

4 *Ask the Archangel Metatron to watch over them and keep them safe. You can also ask him to help them gain wisdom and knowledge.*

5 *Take your time and remember to thank the Archangel Metatron when he is finished. When you feel ready, open your eyes.*

The Guardian Angel, *in the style of Horace Vernet, 19th century, ceramic plaque.*

The 70 Amulet Angels

An amulet containing the names of 70 Angels, which are invoked at the time of a mother giving birth, will give both a mother and her newborn child protection from the evil eye and sorcery. Some names are repeated:

Michael, Gabriel, Raphael, Nuriel, Kidumiel, Malkiel, Tzadkiel, Padiel, Zumiel, Chafriel, Zuriel, Ramuel, Yofiel, Sturi(el), Gazriel, Udriel, Lahariel, Chaskiel, Rachmiel, Katzhiel, Schachniel, Karkiel, Ahiel, Chaniel, Lahal, Machiel, Shebniel, Rachsiel, Rumiel, Kadmiel, Kadal, Chachhmiel, Ramal, Katchiel, Aniel, Azriel, Chachmal, Machnia, Kaniel, Griel or Grial, Tzrtak, Ofiel, Rachmiel, Sensenyha, Udrgazyia, Rsassiel, Ramiel, Sniel, Tahariel, Yezriel, Neria(h), Samchia (Samchiel), Ygal, Tsirya, Rigal, Tsuria, Psisya, Oriel, Smachia, Machnia, Kenunit, Yeruel, Tatrusia, Chaniel, Zechrel, Variel, Diniel, Gdiel or Gediel, Briel, Ahaniel.

Education and Creativity

The Archangel Jophiel is also known as the Angel of illumination. All ideas, perception, and

Archangel of illumination

The Archangel Jophiel works with the Yellow Ray of illumination and wisdom, and this short exercise can help you connect with him:

1 *Take yourself to a quiet place, sit comfortably, relax, and concentrate on your breathing.*

2 *When you feel fully relaxed, visualize as you inhale that you are breathing in the Yellow Ray of the Archangel Jophiel. Visualize it filling every part of you.*

3 *Now invoke the Archangel Jophiel to connect with you, asking him to grant you the gifts of*

wisdom, understanding, and creativity. Try to feel his energy beside you. If you need help with a problem or feel low or depressed, ask him to help you. If you feel that your creative juices are blocked, ask him to clear them.

4 *When you are finished, remember to thank the Archangel Jophiel and be attentive to any message he may have for you. Be aware of him leaving your side and the Yellow Ray leaving your body slowly at the same time as you exhale your breath.*

5 *When you are ready, open your eyes.*

knowledge stem from him, and he can help us to discover abilities we did not know we possessed. He can inspire our thirst for knowledge and creativity, while simultaneously encouraging our development for the highest good. For overcoming feelings of depression and low self-esteem, his help is invaluable.

Love and Relationships

The Archangel Chamuel is in charge of love and relationships, and it is he from whom you should request help if you have problems in this area. Call upon the Archangel Chamuel if you want to find a new loving relationship, either romantic or platonic, or new like-minded friends. Once these are found, the Archangel Chamuel will help you build and sustain your relationships. You can also invoke the Archangel Chamuel if you need assistance in repairing any misunderstandings.

Moving on with Your Life

It is sometimes very hard to get on with our lives when there are feelings that attach us to the past, or to other people. We need to call upon the Archangel Michael to help us cut the psychic ties that bind us to events, times, places, and relationships. We may also need to cut our emotional ties with someone trying to control our lives—it could be a partner, colleague, or perhaps even a mother. Throughout our lives we bond emotionally with numerous people. This is great while a relationship is on an even footing, but if it breaks down—for whatever reason—you may feel that you cannot get on with your life because this person still has a hold over you. You may also realize that certain people tend to make you feel depressed, negative, or drained when you are in contact with them.

In the "Freedom from negativity" exercise on pages 70–71, we connect with the Archangel Michael, who can help us cut the ties that bind us to other people, places, or events, allowing us to clear the clutter of negative influences. This may include unwanted aspects of ourselves that we know are not healthy, or a fear deeply rooted within our psyche that rears its ugly head

Freedom from negativity

Connect with the Archangel Michael for help in breaking unhealthy emotional ties.

1 *Take yourself to a quiet place where you will not be disturbed, or to your sacred space (see page 80). Remove your shoes and place your feet firmly on the floor. Relax; close your eyes.*

2 *Concentrate on your breathing. Breathe in for a count of four through your nose, then exhale through your mouth for a count of four. Now visualize that there are roots growing down through the ground from the soles of your feet. As you breathe they are growing deeper and deeper, anchoring you to the ground. Now, as you breathe in visualize that you are inhaling the Blue Ray of the Archangel Michael. As you exhale, you are expelling any stress or negative thoughts.*

3 *When you are ready, invoke the Archangel Michael to be with you. Try to feel his presence—be aware of perhaps a slight tingle in your arms, a slight brush against your arm, or a comforting feeling of warmth.*

4 *Now appeal to the Archangel Michael to cover you with his protective cloak, so that nothing can harm you and you feel secure and loved. Imagine this cloak covering you. It may feel solid or it could be light and pliable like a blue cloud—this is your meditation so whatever feels right for you is best.*

5 *Think about the negative influences in your life and ask Archangel Michael to cut the cords that are binding them to you. Visualize a cord reaching from within you, connecting to whatever or whoever is holding you back.*

every now and then. Archangel Michael represents strength in body and spirit. Many people visualize him wearing a cloak of cobalt blue and rescuing us with his sword. This can be metal—or a flame—whichever is preferred, and can cut the fear and unhelpful emotions out of our lives. His cloak can shield us from harmful negative energies.

Physical Healing

Call upon the Archangel Raphael for all types of healing, both for yourself and for others. When invoking him, visualize breathing in his Green Ray for self-healing. If sending out healing to others, visualize this Green Ray connecting with them, infusing them with its healing energy.

Visualize him taking his sword of metal or flame and cutting straight through the cord to set you free. Feel that he has cut away the darkness, negativity, and perhaps fear that has been holding you back and preventing you from getting on with your life.

6 *Now that the negative influences are cut away, ask Michael to help you grow emotionally, physically, and spiritually stronger.*

Ask him to guide you to have love, patience, and wisdom to deal with new people and situations that are in your life now or about to enter it.

Remain constantly aware of his cloak around you, shielding you from danger and harm.

Ask the Archangel Michael if he has anything that he would like to advise you about or tell you.

7 *When you feel ready, thank the Archangel Michael and visualize his cloak being removed from around you as he leaves you.*

Concentrate once again on your breathing. Visualize the Blue Ray of the Archangel Michael vaporize with each outgoing breath. Now be aware of the roots that grew out of the soles of your feet retracting back to where they came from.

8 *Become aware of your physical body; when you feel ready, open your eyes. Stand up and take a moment to become fully aware of your surroundings.*

Wisdom and Self-Esteem

We all have insecurities that every now and then nag away at us. Many of these probably began years ago, when perhaps our parents, teachers, or partners made us feel that we had done something wrong, or perhaps we were made to feel that our achievements were never good enough. If we dwell on negative thoughts, it can hold us back from achieving the good things in life. In extreme cases, it may also lead to physical illness. The Angel Zagzagel is the Angel of wisdom, who can be called upon to help you to deal with insecurities from the past or present. Zagzagel can give you the wisdom and self-esteem to think positively about the future.

PART 2

Communicating with Angels

when someone invites their Angels to converse with them, all the Angelic Hierarchies rejoice.

Annunciatory Angel, *Fra Angelico, 1450–55, gold leaf and tempera on wood panel, Detroit Institute of Arts, USA. Bequest of Eleanor Clay Ford/The Bridgeman Art Library.*

Inviting Angels into Your Life

When the time is right Angels will enter your life.
It may be that you have reached the right stage
of your spiritual development and you are consciously
inviting them to connect with you, or perhaps you
have reached out to them in a time of deepest
despair. In this chapter we will examine the many
ways you can work towards having the blissful
experience of connecting and working with your Angels.

Self-transformation

PERSONAL GROWTH

Life is not easy! We have all suffered setbacks, problems, and sometimes the depths of despair. However, we must remember that we are put on this Earth to learn specific lessons as part of our spiritual growth. According to Kabbalist teaching, when we were created we each appeared before God who instructed us as to our destiny—what our physical life journey was to accomplish. Although reluctant to descend into what one Kabbalist called this "Vale of Tears" the answer was "It was for this you were called, created, formed, and made."

The confidence that we show the outside world often masks an inner need for love, security, and self-belief. It is this submerged part of our personality, where we hide the unacknowledged aspects of ourselves— what Carl Jung called our shadow—that we must learn to embrace. By learning to understand ourselves, we can grow emotionally, mentally, and spiritually. We need to learn to acknowledge our shortcomings—such as self-pity, anger, and envy—as it is the balance of our positive and negative attributes that make us the people we are. You do not have to be perfect to be worthy of Angelic communication. Nothing could be further from the truth! Our Angels love us unconditionally for who and what we are.

THE DARK NIGHT OF THE SOUL

Many people embarking on a journey to raise their spiritual consciousness go through what is called the "dark night of the soul." This journey through the "dark night" often occurs after considerable advancement toward higher consciousness. Or, like my own personal "dark night," it is a way of pushing you into the right direction for your own personal spiritual growth. It is always a turning point in our lives.

My "dark night of the soul" changed my world, and the way I think and act, forever. I was very lucky that I was born with a spiritual knowledge, which was encouraged by my late father who also understood and carried out healing, divination, and many other forms of oral Kabbalah practice. However, we lived in London in the 1950s where it was difficult to find other people open to this type of spirituality. As I felt out of sync with my peer group I rarely discussed my knowledge and in many ways felt compelled to hide it from others. I got married at 22, had three beautiful daughters, and became a full-time housewife until they grew up and I went to college. However, although I loved doing my history degree, I felt a strong urge to work at a spiritual level and I found myself questioning my life's purpose. In the meantime my husband had become a successful businessman, founding and running a company on the London Stock Exchange. I wanted for nothing, but I was not happy. I knew that I was supposed to be doing something else but had no idea what.

My "dark night" arrived suddenly and unexpectedly. Suddenly, the bank called in my husband's company's loan. Not only did my husband lose his company, but we also had personal guarantees against our home. We now had no income and, because the bank gave us no time to sell our house, we had the bailiffs poised to throw us out of our home. At the same time my dyslexic daughter was doing her finals.

Through this period I had to be seen to be strong for the sake of those around me. I found a new house, arranged for the packing to be done, and sorted out as much as I could. At the same time we were having to go to court and losing every hearing, allowing the bank to go after everything we had. Their lawyer always faxed over letters on a Friday evening, so we would worry the whole weekend. We were granted a reasonable period to remortgage our home, but the bank's lawyer appealed and got this cut down to a few weeks so it was impossible to get the paperwork in place. I went through a time of the darkest despair. I could not sleep, I could feel my heart pounding with worry, and I would become short of breath. I felt totally alone and found it impossible to discuss my feelings with other people—including my own family. On occasions I even felt suicidal because the pressure from the bank and their lawyer was relentless.

This period was my "dark night of the soul" although I did not know it at the time. The light had gone out of my life and I felt I was going through the motions of living

Calling of Joan of Arc (Maid of Orleans),
Eugene Thirion, 19th century. akg-images.

day to day in permanent darkness. I felt totally out of sync with everyone around me —after all how can people living normal lives understand what it is like to be hounded out of your home? Toward the end of this period, once we had moved and life became a little better, my spiritual levels began to rise and I became aware of the Angels that were surrounding me. I could hear them as they tried to comfort me and help me to recover from the heartache and problems that I had been through. They began to guide me on how to use my spiritual

Carrying the weight of the world

knowledge and how I could help others. They showed me the way to spiritual growth.

Today I know that my Angels and spiritual guides are always there. I merely have to open up my thoughts to create a direct channel with them. This is the fifth book I have written about spiritual matters and I also give advice and healing on a regular basis. In the year 2000 I put it to my Angels that I needed to earn a better living because I was the main breadwinner in my family; my husband was still fighting for justice from the banks—and still is. Through my Angel's guidance and coincidental meetings with various people I was guided to open a market research company, recruiting people to attend focus groups. This enterprise has grown very quickly and turned out to be very successful.

What my "dark night of the soul" taught me personally was to see the world around me in a different light. I have more feeling for the pain and hurt of others and know that the knowledge with which I came into this life is a great gift to be shared with others. Going through the "dark night of the soul" marks a turning point in our lives in which we can change our attitudes to ourselves and others, and move to a higher level of spiritual transformation.

GETTING STARTED

In order to connect and work with your Angels, you should try to be in an environment where you are free from emotional and physical stress and can feel relaxed. Define some personal space for yourself. This could be a particular room or even your whole home—whatever space you claim is the area to focus on. Even the most spiritually experienced or naturally gifted people need to be able to work in an area where they feel comfortable and will not be disturbed by everyday things like the phone, doorbell, or other noise.

Firstly, get rid of any unnecessary clutter. Piles of old newspapers and magazines will not get any smaller; you need to make up your mind to clear them out. Sort out clothing that you have not worn for years and dispose of it and any other unwanted items, such as old furniture. Once this is done and your area is tidy, make sure it is clean. Having a clean space with no dust will help you breathe easier and is a much healthier environment for the mind, body, and soul.

Now that you have cleaned your home, open the windows daily to let in fresh air and natural light, and to let out stale energy. Sound can break up stagnant energy. Some people use Tibetan bowls or small Tibetan cymbals to get the right resonance; others may use drums or rattles. One of the easiest ways to use sound is simply to clap your hands, especially in the corners where negative energy can lurk.

Smudging

I believe in cleansing my home with smudge sticks on a regular basis. Smudging—a term that originated in the Native American culture—is the burning of herbs or incense for cleansing and purifying. When done correctly it can bring emotional, physical, and spiritual balance. The main herbs used in smudge sticks are sage, cedar, juniper, lavender, and sweet grass—often a mix. Rooms and psychic tools, such as crystals and other objects that hold energy, can be smudged on a regular basis. The main purpose of smudging is to purify a space and to banish any negative vibrations and unwanted energies.

You need to light a smudge stick. I usually hold a small plate under the burning end as I find small parts can fall from it, which can cause damage. The smoke needs to be wafted around the room, especially into the corners. When you have finished, if you have some of the smudge stick left, make sure that it is put out properly—I put it under running water. I leave it to dry, then wrap it up until the next time I want to use it. In our household we also, when smudging, fan the smoke over each family member to clear out any unhealthy energies or vibrations.

MAKING A SACRED SPACE

Many people find it satisfying to make a permanent space in their home where they can find peace and are at ease with themselves. By filling this with articles specifically to help enhance your spiritual vibrations and energy you are making your own sacred space or Angelic altar. Every time you use your special place, some of the energy created when you meditate or concentrate on contacting your Angels will linger. This makes it easier each time you return to open yourself up to spiritual and Angelic forces. You may find that, as you evolve along this pathway, in time, you will not need to meditate. You may find you only have to enter your sacred space, relax, and think of your intentions, to become an open channel to the Angelic realms. They will be able to flood you with their energies within seconds or minutes.

Let your Angels guide you to the items you want to place in this personal space. Remember that the space will affect your mind and senses; it is where you will feel

Angel Musician, *Melozzo da Forli,*
15th century, fresco, Vatican Museums and
Galleries, Vatican City, Italy. Giraudon/The
Bridgeman Art Library.

balanced, happy, and secure and where you will be open to the peace, love, and harmony of your Angels. Keep your space clean and warm, and include somewhere comfortable to sit. This could be an armchair, or you may prefer some large pillows on the floor. Remember, though, in most meditations, it is important that the soles of your bare feet touch the floor so that you are "grounded" to the Earth when meditating.

Check that your lighting is not too harsh and that you can adjust it to make it right for you. There is nothing better than natural light coming in through a window, but this may not be possible or we may only be able to carry out spiritual work once it is dark. If you are going to use candles and incense make sure that you can air this space frequently. Here are some suggestions for your space but the most important thing is that the ambience is exactly right for you:

Mini Disk or iPod

Many people I have met record favorite meditations or visualizations from my books, which they keep in easy reach within their sacred space.

Music

You may like to play relaxing music when meditating and there are many options for you to choose from. Some people like to listen to relaxing classical music, while others prefer New Age music, including Tibetan or Gregorian chants, South American pan pipes, or dolphin songs. There are also a number of specific compilations of Angelic music available. For others, like myself, music can be a distraction rather than a harmonious helper. I prefer silence when channeling or healing.

Color

Color is a key stimulator for both body and soul, as discussed in *Angels and Color* on page 116. Introducing color appropriately into your sacred space will help raise the energy and vibrational levels within. This can be done in a number of ways:

Cut flowers The fragrance and color of freshly cut flowers offer a wonderful way in which to add natural enhancement to your sacred space.

Candles Burning candles is particularly useful in stilling the mind when meditating. The color of your candles can contribute

Flowers for your sacred space

and spirituality—or any crystal that appeals instantly to you. See *Working with Crystals* on page 140.

Scent

Burning incense or aromatherapy oil to work through your sense of smell is useful in helping you to relax. The part of your brain that detects smell is very closely linked to your emotional center.

The following is a selection of some of the readily available aromatherapy oils that can help you to relax: cedarwood, chamomile, sage, rosemary, geranium, jasmine, lavender, lemongrass, orange, rose, rosewood, sandalwood, and vanilla.

You may wish to use fragranced candles, particularly incense, potpourri, or sprays—or even plug-in air fresheners.

powerfully to the nature of the contact you need with your Angels. See *Angels and Working with Candles* on page 135.

Crystals These are energy transmitters and I always feel it is important to have your favorite crystals around you when working with the Angelic and spiritual realms. If you are choosing crystals for the first time I would suggest clear quartz, which is a powerful energy-amplifier, and amethyst, for healing

Angel Message Cards

Many people like to keep their Angel Message cards in their sacred space. When starting to work with your Angels you may wish to take one of your cards at random and concentrate on the message for a while to get you started. If you have my Guardian Angel cards, you may wish to concentrate your thoughts on connecting with one of the

Archangels that this pack is dedicated to. If so, have the card of your chosen Archangel laid out in front of you so that it can help you concentrate (see *Using Angel Message Cards* on page 88).

Angel Journal or Angel Diary

Most people forget their experiences and feelings with time. If you write down your Angelic encounters as they happen, you will have a tangible record to keep forever. Keeping an Angel journal or Angel diary is your own personal way of documenting your Angelic experiences. Dreams should also be written down as soon as possible, as they are easily forgotten. Doing this will give you the opportunity to ask your Angels to help you find the hidden meaning of your dreams when meditating or invoking them.

Any kind of notebook will do, but many will prefer to look for one that they find particularly beautiful. You can also use your journal or diary for many personal things such as:

- To record your dreams and visions.
- To record memorable and happy occasions.
- To keep photos of your loved ones and your favorite Angel pictures.

Calcite comes in many colors—just a few are shown here: (from left to right) orange, yellow, pink, green, and orange calcite.

Keeping an Angel journal

- To keep a note of the different meditations you have used and your feelings about them.
- To keep notes and pictures of inspirational people.
- To illustrate the pages with drawings and sketches.
- Keeping and perusing a journal will help make your connection with your Angels stronger and more powerful by focusing your mind, stilling your thoughts, and attracting the love and peace of your Angels.

Personal Items

You may want to place photographs of people or places that are meaningful to you in your sacred space , as well as perhaps Angel pictures, Angel jewelry, or shells that you have collected on seaside holidays and which have happy memories for you. You may have an assortment of other items that you have collected over time that mean a lot to you and make you feel happy, relaxed, and peaceful. If you do not have the space for a permanent Angel altar or sacred space, collect your special items— such as crystals—and arrange them in a pretty box so that it is easy to spread them around you when you are ready to work with them.

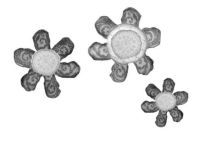

A Natural Sacred Space

There is nothing nicer than being able to open up to your Angels surrounded by nature. If you are living in a temperate climate then you will have more opportunity to do this than those of us living in countries with more extreme weather. It may take a little time to get used to meditating outside, but persevere —it is worth it! As you get used to channeling your Angels while surrounded by the natural world, so you will also become sensitive to using your Angel's energies and love for healing on a planetary level.

By creating a sacred space in your own garden you can incorporate the elements to add more energy. The elements of Earth and air will already be present and—if it is a sunny day—fire will also be represented.

Making a sacred space

Flowers for spiritual energy

If you do not have a water feature in your garden, you can add water, the fourth element, by placing a bowl of water near you as you meditate.

You can also help to raise the spiritual energy in your garden by growing a variety of herbs and flowers. For herbal inspiration, plant lavender to help you relax, sage for its cleansing properties, rosemary to enhance mental clarity, and mint to help clear your mind and from which to make a refreshing and healthy drink.

Choose flowering plants that provide the color you wish to surround yourself with. Some, particularly those that provide pollen for bees or berries for birds, will attract wildlife into your garden. This will enhance your respect for all living things as well as your experience of the balance of nature. Honeysuckle, roses, hyacinth, gardenias, jasmine, and lilac are particularly powerful, both for their color and fragrance, when helping you to connect with your Angels.

USING ANGEL MESSAGE CARDS

The "Angel Message" cards and "Guardian Angels" cards, published by Cico Books and written in the form of affirmations, are powerful tools to help your communication with Angels. Both sets of cards are channeled messages, which have proven to be a great source of help and comfort to the many people who have used them. They work well because they act as a subtle device to awaken and shift the power of your subconscious mind, helping you connect first with your soul and then with your Angels.

I have met many, many people who have used these cards and who tell me that they always seem to relate to something that is happening to them at the time. I have no idea how or why this is. All I know is that when I open up to my Angels and work with them writing these affirmations, their words pour into my mind. The cards are a tool to be used for opening communication with Angels. They will first focus you so you can connect with your spiritual essence, then open a channel to the vibrations and energies of the Cosmos.

There are a number of ways in which to use the cards successfully; it is always best to use them instinctively in the way that feels right for you personally. One popular way to use them is to choose a time when feeling relaxed and ready to communicate with your Angels. Pick as many as you want, one at a time, concentrating on each individual message. Feel yourself open up to your Angels and feel their energies around you. Try to hear them in your heart and head.

The Guardian Angel cards are a tool to center your mind and then link you specifically with your Guardian and Archangels. If you have a particular problem, the cards in the Angel Messages pack are color coded so you can use the cards that relate to the area of your life that you want to concentrate on. You have yellow cards for career guidance, ideas, and creativity, pink for love and relationships, purple for spiritual

38

Peaceful thoughts
create a path
of light
for your angels.

development and transformation, and blue-green for healing on a personal and global level. These are divided into messages for love, healing, wisdom, and peace. Using these cards in your sacred space or at your Angelic altar will help to raise your level of consciousness so that Angels can connect with you.

Katerina Nicolaou writes: I first started using the Angel Message cards when both I and my best friend bought a pack each. It was not until weeks later when I was going through a very difficult and stressful period of my life—I literally just picked them up, I shuffled them, and I asked a question in my head of what was bothering me. I was so surprised when on the first card I lifted, the message on it rang absolutely true to my situation at the time. This did not happen just once. I started to use them once a week to give me support and comfort. The card I chose I would leave by my bedside before I went to sleep. In the morning I would read it through again so it would give me encouragement and support for the day.

I do not believe it was just coincidence. I truly believe this was my Angels linking to me through the cards to give a feeling of love and support through the difficult times. The strange thing that I have always found is that the message that I pick is always, without fail, about whatever problem is bothering me at the time. Sometimes friends would upset me, or family, or sometimes my relationships. The cards always relate to my problems—it is unbelievable!

Ways to Use Your Cards

There are no right or wrong ways to use your cards; just use your intuition and what feels right for you. Here are some suggestions I find useful: Keep your cards in a dish and pick one out at random. Concentrate upon the message then place it where you will see it regularly. Lay the cards out in front of you, ask a question, and then pick up one and see what the message it holds means to you. Shuffle your cards, cut them three times, and then pick up the top card and read and absorb the message. Every time you feel you need inspiration or have a question, pick a card randomly.

Some of you may prefer using the books that come with both packs of cards. These contain a simple, basic message as well as a much longer, more detailed version of it. With your eyes either open or closed, flick through the book or just open it up randomly and read the message on the page you have happened upon.

Whichever method you use, if you need to send out healing thoughts to others concentrate on the message to help you link to your Angels and then, with their help, visualize sending out your healing thoughts.

Using Your Angel Message Cards for Divination

The Angel Message cards can also be used for divination as their messages facilitate connection with our "inner-self" and our Angels. This simple spread is one that will show the dominant influences in your past, present, and future. If using the "Angel Message" cards, the colors of the cards that appear in the four positions are an important factor of what is, was, and will be influencing your life. You can use this layout to ask questions or to give guidance. Before you begin, hold the cards and think of what you are looking for. When using Angel Message cards for divination, I normally shuffle them and then cut the pack three times, dealing from the top. The following layout, with Card 2 placed across Card 1, is ideal for obtaining Angelic guidance about what life has in store for you:

Card 1 shows your present circumstances.
Card 2 reveals what is crossing over your present situation.
Card 3 looks at what is past and moving out of your life.
Card 4 is your future and what lies ahead of you as you move on with your life.

Card 3

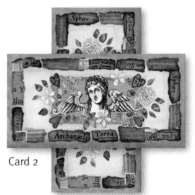

Card 2

Card 1

Card 4

Dowsing Your Angel Affirmations

Dowsing is a simple technique that is used to detect flows of energy. Many people enjoy dowsing for their affirmation or message for the day. You can either buy a pendulum, which is usually made from metal, crystal or wood, or make one yourself. If you want to make your own, you can attach either a small personal item, such as a ring or a crystal, to a piece of cord. If using a crystal, wash it first to clear any negative memories. This is not necessary for a piece of personal jewelry.

Every time you use your pendulum it is essential that you tune it in. Hold it above the palm of your hand and ask it to show you the way it will swing for "yes." It may start to swing clockwise, counterclockwise, or backward, and forward. Once you have ascertained the direction for "yes" you will need to repeat this to find "no." You may find that the next time you use the pendulum, all of the directions have changed—this is perfectly normal.

Now hold your pendulum above a selection of Angel Message cards—perhaps six or eight—and let it choose your affirmation by asking yes and no above each one. When your pendulum demonstrates yes, turn over this card and meditate on it. Many also use this technique without using an affirmation.

MEDITATION

Meditation is the discipline by which we learn to control the mind to think in an organized manner. In our normal state of mind we bounce from one thought to another as we receive external sensory stimuli. As a result, we may react in an uncontrolled way, emotionally and/or physically. When we meditate, we learn to control our mind and thoughts. In our normal state we are usually only conscious of our physical existence but, through meditation,

we learn to control first our conscious mind, then our subconscious. It is through connecting with the subconscious part of our mind that we begin to truly know ourselves. This is a vital aspect of our developmental journey into spiritual beings.

The main aim of meditation is to reach a "higher state of consciousness." This is a difficult state to explain, but put simply it means we are aiming to use a particular part of our mind that has no conscious access. Most forms of meditation begin with the discipline of breathing control through exercises. Breathing is normally an automatic function that is controlled by our unconscious mind so, by first concentrating on our breathing, we are expediting a crossover from our conscious to our unconscious mind.

Throughout my books I use meditations to help you reach this higher state of consciousness. I usually suggest that you sit on a chair so that your feet can rest on the floor, since I feel it is important that you are "grounded." To do this I always ask that you remove your shoes, place your feet flat on the floor, and visualize strong roots growing out of the soles of your feet, anchoring you securely to the Earth. This is my preferred method because, even when I was young

and had never heard of meditation, it was my clairsentient (see page 100) instinct to always remove my shoes and to do my healing barefooted. I have always had the instinct that, because I was working with the spiritual realms, it was also important that I was grounded to the Earth.

Some of you, however, may prefer to sit cross-legged or perhaps in the lotus position. Another comfortable way to meditate is to lie on your back on the floor. Whichever way comes naturally to you will be the best way so long as you are warm and relaxed. Be aware that during meditation your body temperature can sometimes drop a little so make sure that you do not get cold. Choose a place where you will not be disturbed. You may need to switch off your cellphone to make sure it does not ring. Play some soothing music if you wish. If you are just starting out it may be a good idea to use a short, guided meditation so you do not have to think what you need to do next.

It is very important that all meditations are finished properly. Always read the directions and make sure that all the steps leading to opening yourself up are reversed when closing yourself down. I talk from experience, as many years ago I went to a workshop for healers but had to leave early to get to a funeral. Unfortunately, in my hurry, I did not close down properly and when I was with my friend – who had lost her mother – I picked up all of her feelings of sorrow and grief.

Raising Conscious Awareness

This meditation exercise will raise your levels
of consciousness and help you learn to
ground yourself.

1 *Sit in a comfortable chair in an area where
you will not be disturbed. Remove any
footwear and place the soles of your feet flat
on the floor.*

2 *Concentrate on your breathing. Breathe in
through your nose for a count of four and out
through your mouth for a count of four.
Close your eyes and focus your attention on
your body. Beginning with your feet, slowly
move your attention up through your legs,
thighs, torso, arms, through to your
fingertips, neck, and then your head; feel
yourself relax throughout.*

3 *Now visualize that you are surrounded by
light. As you breathe in, inhale this light and
feel it filling your entire body. As you breathe
out, exhale all the tension and pain that you
feel throughout your body.*

*Inhale light, exhale tension—if your mind
begins to wander, bring your attention back
to your breathing and focus on it.*

4 *When you feel ready, visualize that you
have strong roots growing from the soles of
your feet, pushing their way into the ground
below, no matter how many floors up you may
be. Visualize them burrowing into the Earth.*

5 *When you next inhale, visualize the energy
of the Earth being sucked up through the
roots into your body. With each breath
imagine more and more of the Earth's energy
entering you, working its way slowly up
through your feet, toes, legs, torso, arms,
fingers, neck, and head, until it fills every
part of you.*

6 *Visualize that the crown of your head has
an opening and through it rays of energy are
reaching up to the sky and then out farther
into the Cosmos.*

*As you inhale, visualize the energy
of the Cosmos being drawn into your mind,
head, and body through these rays and feel
it gradually filling every part of you.*

7 *Now breathe in the two energies together.
Inhale both the energy coming up through
you from the Earth, while at the same time feel
the energy of the Cosmos filling your mind
and heart.*

*Bathe in these energies for as long as
you like. You are now connected to both the
Universe and the Earth.*

8 *Ask your Angels to enter your life and to fill
and surround you with their gifts of
love, peace, tranquility, and joy. Sense your
Angels connecting with you and bathe in the
wonderful feeling it brings—stay in this place
for as long as you want.*

9 When you are ready to close down, thank your Angels for their gifts and again focus on your breathing. Feel the energy of the Cosmos retreat from your body, back through its linking rays. Feel its connection with your body dissolve and visualize the opening in your crown close. Now feel the energy that has filled you from the Earth descend back down from your head, neck, fingers, arms, torso, thighs, legs, through to your feet.

Now visualize the energy going back down to its place of origin, through the roots that have been anchoring you to the Earth.

Visualize the roots that have been growing from the soles of your feet dissolving away.

10 Concentrate on your breathing and become aware of your body and where you are sitting. Become aware of your heartbeat and the sounds around you. Take your time; when you are ready open your eyes.

OPENING UP TO ANGELIC COMMUNICATION

Many people have asked me how they will know when they are ready to communicate with their Angels. Don't worry, you will! Your Angels have been patiently waiting for you to reach the right stage of your spiritual progress in this lifetime and for you to invite them into your life. As the veils between our worlds become thinner, as people seek increasingly to link with the Universal Consciousness, so it becomes easier to sense Angels.

Once you have taken the practical, physical steps—such as cleansing your environment, and using tools such as crystals and color—toward linking to your Angels, you need to prepare yourself mentally and emotionally. Your aim is to start using your subconscious mind. A simple way to describe this is to think of your mind as a radio; it needs to be retuned to a new frequency so that you can open a channel of communication to your Angels.

Feeling Your Angels Connecting with You

Through channeling, your Angels will be able to speak to you in a language you are familiar with and can understand. There are lots of ways that people can become aware of Angels. Many, totally unexpectedly, go through profound changes in the way they think and act as they become sensitive to the energies of their Angels. Most people never actually see an Angel, but there are many ways in which they can alert you to their existence. Following are some of the telltale signs of Angelic presence.

Welcoming Angel

Feathers Many people find a white feather that has appeared from nowhere and instinctively know that it is a sign from their Angels. If this happens to you, keep your white feather safe to help you connect with your Angels.

Synchronicity Our Angels often use coincidence and synchronicity to make us aware of them, or as a nudge to confirm their presence. You may be thinking of your Angels in general or you may be thinking about the name of your Guardian Angel, when over a short period of time you hear things on the radio or television, or even from friends, that you can link to this. You may even see a billboard with a name that keeps repeating itself. Take these as a sign of the name of your Angel.

Some years ago, a couple of days after my publisher had contacted me about writing a new book on Angels, I asked my Angels why, although I channel their messages and can feel their energies in many different ways, I had never seen them or received the gift of a white feather. It was the weekend of my eldest daughter's wedding and probably the stress was beginning to get to me—especially as the new book proposal had to be ready within two days. Within minutes the doorbell rang and a beautiful bouquet of large blooms was delivered. Unbelievably, the label on the envelope simply stated "Angel Flowers." It was as if my Angels were saying to me "Well, you wanted proof and now you have it!"

Flowers Sometimes you will find that flowers will last longer when placed on an Angelic altar or in your sacred space. I have also been told of potted plants that have unexpectedly reflowered when put in these places.

Fragrance When meditating or thinking of your Angels a beautiful fragrance can suddenly waft unexpectedly through the room.

Sensation During meditation, when you have invoked your Angels, you may feel a tingling sensation around your body or going through your hands like a gentle electric current. If you then ask your Angels to show you that this is their energy you may feel the tingling change slightly in nature.

Unexpected Gifts There are many Angelic items available today. If someone, unprompted, thinks to buy you one, take it as a sign that your Angels have nudged them toward this purchase.

Sandra T. wrote to me of her experience:

I received an e-mail from our mutual friend Jonathan regarding your book and I would like to share with you an experience I had only yesterday—but let's start at the beginning. I had been feeling down the last few days. I had met up with two friends on Saturday, 16th December and we had gone to Thameside for the "Frost Fair" and a visit to the Globe Theatre—all proceeds for the day going to charity.

My two friends have very recently "got it together" which in turn reminded me of a close relationship I had had this time last year, which started me feeling sorry for myself. This, coupled with my sight impairment, really got to me and in the evening—alone by choice and not speaking to anyone—I decided to give myself some Reiki healing and pray to my Angel friends asking them for a big hug. I always feel spiritual when I give Reiki healing.

Anyway, yesterday I received a "blanket" e-mail from Jonathan asking if anyone had had Angel experiences then they should write to you and I said to myself, "Well, I

Mignon, *Wilhelm von Schadow, 1825–28, oil on canvas, Museum der Bildenden Künste, Leipzig, Germany. akg-images.*

haven't had an Angel experience" and I thought no more about it as I continued to cook my dinner. Later on a friend was coming to me. I was to give her an Indian Head Massage, so I thought I would light some incense to get rid of the smell of cooking.

As I went to fetch the incense I noticed a tiny Angel at the corner of a framed certificate I had. I picked up the frame and underneath lay another tiny Angel. My first reaction was "Oh my God, where did they come from?" to be followed by "It must have been my friend who put them there—she knows how I love Angels." Well I shared this story with my friend Sue and told her my "explanation." It was some time later that evening before I spoke to my friend Noreen, and of course I thanked her for my tiny Angels. But here's the thing—SHE KNEW NOTHING ABOUT THEM!

I do not know from whence they came. I even started questioning myself: "Did I find them somewhere and forgot about it?" But of course I would have remembered something so recent. I like to believe they heard my prayer and sent me a sign—who knows? There is certainly no other explanation!

THE SIX SPIRITUAL SENSES

You can also receive spiritual communication, information, love, and guidance through one of your six spiritual senses.

Clairvoyance

The word "clairvoyant" means "clear seeing." Many people have the gift whereby their Angels communicate with them through visual images or a series of pictures that appear in their minds. This can be experienced as a picture that suddenly appears in your mind, with or without your eyes closed. You can then dwell upon this image until its meaning becomes clear.

Clairsentience

This means "clear feeling." A clairsentient can sense energies around a person, place, or thing and receive guidance or feelings through their intuition or "gut feeling." The "gut feeling" in question is exactly that—it is centered in your solar plexus, where you can pick up very strong feelings that sometimes feel like you have been punched in the stomach. The other feeling that they can pick up is when you meet someone who makes you feel like the hair on the back of your head is standing up.

Detail from the Annunciation showing the Angel Gabriel, *Fra Angelico, Museo Diocesano, Cortona, Italy. The Bridgeman Art Library.*

My husband has noticed this happen with me a couple of times and has told me that my whole demeanor seems to change when I get very bad "vibes" about someone —which always turns out to be correct! I have worked with this gift since childhood. When I am working with my Angels and spiritual guides doing healing, I often get waves of energy or heat coming down my arms through my fingers. They sometimes alternate with a feeling of electrical currents.

The patient who I am working on normally feels these sensations in the different areas that are being healed.

Claircognizance

Or "clear knowing." This is the gift of having spiritual knowledge without knowing how. Since childhood I have realized that I had a special gift, whereby I had been born with a spiritual knowledge that is not available to most. I had never read about it—I just simply knew and understood it. From quite a young age I was aware of opening myself up to my Angels and spiritual guides and feeling their energy. I considered this to be perfectly normal —I thought that everyone automatically could do healing, use their intuition, understand divination, and translate their dreams.

Clairaudience

"Clear hearing" is the ability to hear in a paranormal manner. This could mean actual sound, but it also refers to the gift of an impression of sound similar to the way in which people can think words without having auditory impressions. When my Angels are channeling their messages to me, this is the way I receive them and one message after the other comes into my mind. Sometimes when writing I may take a break and take a "power nap." However, I think my Angels take great delight in waking me with more messages so that I have to quickly get up in order to get them written down before I forget them!

Clairscentist

This means "clear scent" and there are people who are able to smell fragrances that emanate from the Angelic or spiritual realms. I have had many reports from people who tell me that they can sense when their Angel is with them because they smell, from nowhere, a particular fragrance.

Clairgustant

Or "clear taste." People with this gift are able to psychically taste a substance, such as a particular food or drink, without actually putting anything in their mouth. It can also include the smell of food.

OTHER WAYS THAT WE CAN HEAR OUR ANGELS

There are many ways in which your Angels will try to catch your attention. Here are just a few:

● Out of nowhere you hear some beautiful Heavenly music—sometimes accompanied by Angelic choirs singing.

● You hear someone inside your head calling your name.

● Angels come constantly to your attention—such as in books, advertisements, or seeing Angelic products in shops.

● You turn on the radio or television randomly to find a discussion about Angels.

● You lose something and pray for help, then you look somewhere you would not normally have thought of and the article is there.

Something may even occur to bring Angels into your life, as happened to me recently: I had taken some time out of my spiritual and Angelic work because my market research business had taken off. I was even working on Sundays to catch up with the paperwork. My husband and I went to Greece for a short vacation and, while there, I suddenly felt inspired to do some more

writing. When I returned I realized that my Angels and spiritual guides were active, because suddenly I had lots of people contacting me for healing. The energies I was channeling were very strong and I was also having lots of clairvoyant episodes—small things, really, such as thinking of an actress who had been written out of a television series and then seeing her on television the next time I watched. I would think of a client who I had not spoken to for a while and, within minutes, he or she would phone me.

I then began to think of my publisher, Cindy, who I had last seen at Christmas. I had a strong feeling to contact her and make a lunch date. That, of course, got pushed aside as I have to admit I am a bit of a workaholic and my workload got the better of me. Within a couple of weeks I received a phone call from Cindy, who invited me to work on a synopsis for a new book. All I had to do was sit at my computer and within a very short period of time this was done, channeled through by my Angels, and you are reading the result!

An Angel Playing a Flageolet, *Sir Edward Burne-Jones, 1878, watercolor, gouache, and gold on paper, Sudley House, National Museum, Liverpool, UK. Bridgeman Art Library.*

INVOKING ANGELS

Angels are God's helpers and messengers. Their connection with us on Earth is a gift from the Creator to help us to grow spiritually and to eventually understand the very reason for our being. In times gone past, spiritual seekers would spend many years praying, fasting, and meditating in order to be in a position to receive and understand spiritual experiences. Today, as more and more people around the world are becoming more spiritually aware, the whole vibrational energy level of our planet is being raised, making it far easier for our Angels to connect to us and vice versa.

THE HIGHER SELF

As you commence your spiritual journey of self-awareness and growth, so you learn to connect with your Higher Self. Kabbalah teaches that if we are only using our five physical senses, we are looking at the world around us through a blindfold. The main point of Kabbalah—and most forms of spiritual practice—is that we learn to use our sixth sense and become aware of that "something" at the center of our very being. This has many names including soul, essence, inner self, true self, or nephesh (Hebrew). Many call it our "Higher Self."

This is the part within us that links us to the Cosmos and our Creator. It is through our "Higher Self" that the Angels and the healers of the spiritual realms can truly enter our lives and channel their energies. In order to connect successfully with your Higher Self and then the Angelic realms, you first need to go through a mental process of preparation as set out below:

The Six Steps of Connection

To help you become truly at one with yourself and then to progress to feeling mentally, emotionally, and spiritually at ease and prepared for opening a dialogue with your Angels, I have developed six steps. These should act as a checklist for you to tick as you progress through each of them.

STEP 1 Feel good about yourself Before you can fully get in touch with your inner self, your soul, the first thing you need to do is to feel good about who you are. Learn to love yourself for who you are, not what you are. You are one of God's creations and you were put upon this Earth to grow and develop not only physically and mentally but, more importantly, spritually. We are given our lives on Earth to learn certain lessons that will help our spiritual progress—many call this our Karma.

Take some time at this stage to think about your life—think about how you are going to live it from this point on. As you arrive at a greater understanding of yourself, so will your awareness grow of life around you and that of all living things on this planet. You need to break free from any guilt that is attaching you emotionally to the past. Take a conscious decision to free yourself. For many, guilt is misplaced; it has

Cutting the ties to negative emotions

manifested itself as a habit of self-punishment. There is empowerment through forgiveness and once you have acknowledged and made a positive effort to overcome your faults, you can heal yourself and move on with your life.

STEP 2 Intent To commence opening up a dialogue with your Angels, you should feel excited and comfortable about the prospect. If you are having doubts, visualize that you have already opened up a communication with your Angels and think about how you are feeling about this. If your gut reaction is that you are not sure you should be doing this yet, then it would be better to delay until you are more confident about your feelings.

STEP 3 Purpose It is important to ask and define to yourself why you want to take the step of inviting your Angels into your life. Remember, your Angels cannot and will not interfere with the blueprint of your life. They also cannot help or save you from any stupidity or wrongdoing that you have perpetrated. It is important that you are sure that your intentions and reasons are honorable. Your Angels are waiting for you to communicate with them and will be joyous at giving you their help and love, but

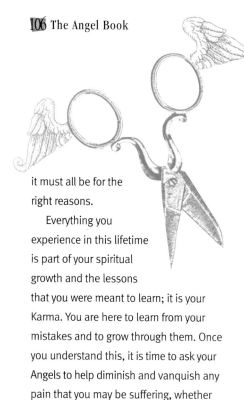

it must all be for the right reasons.

Everything you experience in this lifetime is part of your spiritual growth and the lessons that you were meant to learn; it is your Karma. You are here to learn from your mistakes and to grow through them. Once you understand this, it is time to ask your Angels to help diminish and vanquish any pain that you may be suffering, whether mental or emotional, so that you can move onward with your life.

STEP 4 Focus Now that you have passed through the steps of self-esteem, intent, and purpose, the time has come to focus your mind on how you are going to achieve the next step. This is where you have to work at tuning into your unconscious mind and raising your vibrational levels to a higher level. This is the point where you start to connect and work through the energies of your soul.

As previously discussed in this chapter, there are a number of physical tools that can help you—including crystals and fragrances. Use these together with meditation, which will help you to tune into the spiritual and Angelic dimensions. I have written a number of meditations in this book to help you learn to focus and control your mind, and to help you link to your Higher Self. Once you have worked with these you will be ready to begin working with meditations that are specifically written to invite your Angels into your life.

STEP 5 Communication Having followed the previous steps, you are now ready to become an open channel in order to communicate with your Angels. You will need to work through the methods of meditation discussed in the previous step slowly and methodically, until you are satisfied that you are ready and in control of your mind, emotions, and inner self. As your Angels begin to communicate with you it may be a little "hit and miss." They have been waiting a long time for you to reach this stage in your spiritual development and they will be eager to come and enter your life.

Their vibrational levels are very high and you may need some time before you can raise your own spiritual level high enough to "tune" into them. You may begin by sensing energy shifting around or through you. I myself found that, because my Angels were so happy I was working with them and channeling their messages, they bombarded me with their energy and messages too powerfully to begin with and I was not fully in sync with their power—even though I had been working for many years with spiritual guides. When working on my first collection of Angel Message cards I suffered extremely bad migraines at first, because it took a while for me to become fully adjusted to their vibrations and energies on a physical level.

Today, when working with my Angels—as long as I feel relaxed and am working in an atmosphere that is quiet and warm, and I am not being disturbed—I feel their waves of energy flowing through me, usually starting in my arms and then permeating through my whole body. I ask the questions or I simply wait for their words of wisdom and guidance to come into my mind.

Once you get used to working with your Angels you will be able to ask for their help and wisdom and at the same time let them smother you with their love, compassion, joy, and peace. You can also ask them questions or let them direct you by using your Angel Message cards or even use the method described on page 109 to ask dream questions.

STEP 6 Gratitude It is very important that you always remember to thank your Angels for their presence and for answering your call. They have opened up the channels of communication between the physical world and the Angelic realms sending you their unconditional love and protection. Even if you have gone through the previous steps but have still not been blessed with sensing or hearing your Angels, you should still thank them as they will have heard you—although you may not yet be ready to hear them. As you keep opening up your heart and mind to them and acknowledging their presence it will only be a matter of time before you do.

ASKING YOUR ANGELS QUESTIONS

The most natural way to ask questions is to say them in your mind once you feel you are in contact with your Angelic helpers. Take a moment and then try to hear or feel the answer. You may wish to invoke your Angels by saying something like this:

Please, my Angels, enter my world and help me in my moment of need. I need to know (state your question). Remember to thank your Angels when you have heard an answer.

You may find it easier to do a short meditation as follows:

1 *Sit in your sacred space comfortably, remove your shoes, and place your feet flat on the floor.*

2 *Close your eyes, relax, and concentrate on your breathing. Inhale through your nose for a count of four and exhale through your mouth for a count of four.*

3 *When you feel completely relaxed, invoke your Angels to open a channel of communication with you.*

4 *Now ask your Angel your question, using your heart and mind. Be open to your Angels' connection and any feelings, images, or words that you receive.*

You may wish to write these down so you can contemplate them later.

5 *Remember to thank your Angels. Focus on your breathing, become aware of your body, and open your eyes.*

Some people prefer to write their questions down on a piece of paper, lay it in their sacred space or on their Angelic altar, and concentrate on the written word while awaiting the answer. You may wish to write your question down in your Angel journal, and also the answer when it comes.

Angels and Dream Questions

One of the most ancient and successful ways of asking your Angels questions is through dreams. According to the *Zohar*, one of the

Detail of **The Achievement of Sir Galahad of the Sang Graal Accompanied by Sir Bors and Sir Percival,** *Sir Edward Burne-Jones, 1890, tapestry, London, UK. Sotheby's.*

main books of ancient Kabbalist learning, once the Sun sets and the stars appear a part of our soul leaves our body. This is the reason we begin to feel tired and drained once it becomes night, even if we are still awake. Once we fall asleep, the *Zohar* explains, the main part of the rest of our soul departs our physical body, leaving about 1 percent to sustain us physically. Our soul is now free to ascend back to its place in the Cosmos where it is able, without the constraints of its physical body, to connect freely with the Angels.

Dream incubation has been used for hundreds—if not thousands—of years by mystic practitioners. When we are dreaming our subconscious mind takes over, as we become free from all the constraints of our physical existence. By utilizing and focusing on Angelic communication during this period we can have amazing results. If you have a specific question or are wanting to solve a particular problem and are looking for guidance from your Angels, meditate on it before you go to sleep. Better still, write down your question

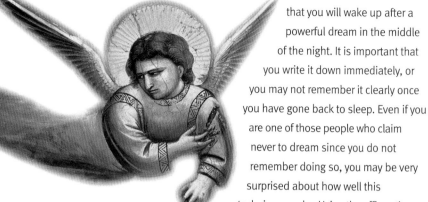

Detail of **The Flight to Egypt**, *Giotto di Bondone, c. 1301–1310, fresco, Arena Chapel, Padua, Italy. akg-images.*

or problem on a piece of paper, meditate on it, and then slip it under the pillow. As you feel yourself relaxing and drifting off to sleep, ask your Angels for help and guidance in finding the answer. You could affirm something like:

Please, my Angels, I beseech you to help me find the answer to my question, which is (say your question) and help me to remember your guidance clearly in the morning. Thank you.

I would suggest that you keep a notebook and pen beside your bed. You may also want a flashlight, if you do not want to switch a bedside light on. There is a very good chance that you will wake up after a powerful dream in the middle of the night. It is important that you write it down immediately, or you may not remember it clearly once you have gone back to sleep. Even if you are one of those people who claim never to dream since you do not remember doing so, you may be very surprised about how well this technique works. Using the affirmation will primarily focus your mind; then, as your subconscious mind takes over, it will shift its spiritual energy to becoming open to your Angels while at the same time making your dreams much more vivid and memorable than normal.

It is not uncommon to have problems with the interpretation of a dream once you are fully awake. The main thing is to realize that you have the answer—sometimes it is easy to work out and sometimes not. The important thing is to try to tune into your intuition so you can work out the answer, which will come to you even though it may take a few minutes, hours, or not until the next day. Very often the answer that you get is totally different to the one that you were expecting—or is something so totally "off the wall" that there is no way you would have thought of it!

CHANNELING MESSAGES FROM YOUR ANGELS

Channeling is the way many of us make a direct connection with our Angels and the spiritual realms, using our conscious awareness. It is a skill that can be developed by most people with the determination to develop and grow spiritually. When you receive spiritual communication, information, and guidance from your Angels they will commune with you in a language that you are familiar with. This can occur when you are meditating, sleeping, writing, feeling inspired, or relaxing, or even when you are doing creative work. Your Angels will usually channel their advice, guidance, and love through one of your spiritual senses (see *The Six Spiritual Senses* on pages 100–101). To become an open channel with your Angels and the spiritual realms, you need first to learn to connect with your inner self. Once you have achieved this, you need to progress to reconnecting with the Universe and ultimately with God.

The easiest way to begin this spiritual journey of learning and connection is usually through meditation. With time, you may not need to meditate but will find that your Angels and guides can come through quickly as soon as you invite them. I have the gift of being an open channel with my Angels and spiritual guides. I merely have to ask them to help with healing or to channel their messages for me to write down, and their energies come flowing through. The only disadvantage of this is sometimes they want my attention when I am busy doing other things. I can be working or out with friends, when suddenly I get waves of heat or electrical currents flowing through me. I then know

An Angel at your shoulder

USING THE ENERGIES OF THE MOON

The phases of the Moon can greatly influence our lives and our spiritual work. Kabbalists and many other spiritual seekers have rarely embarked on important deeds and actions without first having taken into account the phases of the Moon. The New and Full Moon periods are particular periods of intense spiritual and magical focus. The Jewish calendar is based on the lunar passage, with the dates of all the Jewish holidays revolving around the date of the New Moon. In synagogues Rosh Hodesh (the festival of the New Moon) is traditionally celebrated and there is a New-Moon blessing, which should be said in the open air when the New Moon is visible. During the previous Sabbath ceremony the date of the New Moon is always announced and the shofar (ram's horn) is blown as the congregation prays to God to make it a joyous month. The one exception to this is the Sabbath proceeding the month of Tishri when Rosh Hashanah (the Jewish New Year) occurs. The shofar is not blown then in order to fool the Angel of Death, who likes to cause turmoil in people's lives during these festivities.

I always like to program my crystals under the light of a Full Moon. It also can be beneficial when working with your Angels to link the energy of the Moon with what is going on in your life.

New Moon and Waxing Moon

The waxing Moon is the period of about 15 days from the New Moon to the Full Moon, when the Moon is increasing in size. This is the best time for new beginnings; it is during this period that you should begin new endeavors and conceptualize new ideas, such as a new business. It is also a good time to begin a new career, change of job, or study course, or move to a new home—and in times gone by it was considered the best time for a child to begin a new school. This is also a good time for asking for abundance, forgiveness, protection, and increasing your wisdom.

Full Moon

This is the period when the Moon is at its fullest power and the date of the Full Moon each month is noted in many calendars. This is the best time, especially for those less experienced in Angelic communication, to meditate and let the power of the Moon enhance your spiritual development and energy. It is during this period that all communication, both physical and spiritual, is strengthened by natural lunar energy. This is the most powerful period of the month so use it to develop your psychic powers and spiritual knowledge. This is also a good period to forgive yourself and others, use your intuition, be open to communication through dreams, and wish for good things in the future.

Waning Moon

This is the period when the Moon begins to lose its power as it diminishes in size. This period lasts about 15 days from the date of the Full Moon. It is during this period that you should let go of things, break bad habits, move on, and liberate yourself.

ANGEL ENCOUNTERS

Many, many people throughout the world have encounters with Angels that happen unexpectedly and totally out of the blue. Whereas some people are actually lucky enough to see Angels appear to them looking very similar to the ones that we have all grown up with in paintings, others see them in different ways.

Luke writes: My experience of an Angel was when I was 15; the year must have been 1991. I was quite depressed at the time and was in my bedroom after school. It was dark outside so it was in the winter months, as it was not too late in the evening. I remember staring out of my window when I saw an Angel. My Angel was not like the ones I have seen in pictures. My Angel was more like a neon Christmas light Angel and it was strumming a guitar while flying across the sky the same way a plane would except it was not a plane. I know this because, after seeing the Angel, planes did go by, only none of them was an Angel.

There are many recorded instances in which people have had encounters with Angels who appear in the guise of human strangers, appearing unexpectedly and as if from nowhere, in times of danger or distress.

Be not forgetful to entertain strangers, for thereby some have entertained Angels unawares.

HEBREWS 13:2 KING JAMES BIBLE

When I was very young, my parents drove my older sister and me through Spain to get to the coast for a holiday. During the journey a truck crashed into our car and we were stranded in the middle of nowhere. This was the 1950s and it was very hard to find a way to contact someone to get help. My parents were obviously quite worried, as they spoke no Spanish and it seemed that they were marooned with two young children.

Suddenly, from nowhere, a woman suddenly appeared by the car. She spoke English and had a basket of fruit and cold drinks, which she gave us. She told my parents not to worry as she had called a garage. She stayed with us until the tow truck arrived but when my parents went to thank her she had quite simply "vanished."

Detail of
Joachim's Dream,
Giotto di Bondone,
c. 1303–1305, fresco, Arena
Chapel, Padua, Italy. akg-images.

ANGELS AND DREAMS

Another way our Angels can show themselves
to us is through dreams, because they realize
that seeing them appear from nowhere can
often be a frightening experience. One of the
most famous dreams recorded in the *Bible*
was that of Jacob:

And he dreamed, and behold a
ladder set up on the Earth, and the
top of it reached to Heaven: and
behold the angels of God ascending
and descending on it.

GENESIS 28:12 KING JAMES BIBLE

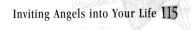

Angels & Color

Most of us use a form of color therapy in our everyday lives without even realizing it. Every color has its own vibration and energy, which can affect us subconsciously even if we are unaware of it at a conscious level.

Once you become aware of this you may realize that your interaction with the world around you differs when you wear clothing or jewelry in particular colors. In a work environment, how often do you put on a suit in a somber black, gray, or navy, to make you feel smart and efficient when you have an important meeting in the office? Or, if you are a young single female going out for the evening, do you dress up in bright, colorful clothes with perhaps some flashy jewelry?

When decorating rooms in their homes or offices, most people are aware that they like to be surrounded by certain colors. These indicate what we need for our current emotional well-being. We are attracted to particular colors whose energies we need to bring into our lives.

As we progress spiritually, we become aware of how important color can be in our lives, and how it can provide a sense of wholeness and well-being. By using color, our channels of communication with our Angels can be accelerated and greatly enhanced.

ANGELS AND THE RAYS

People are becoming increasingly aware of the importance and power of the seven Great Rays of Creation. A Ray is a force or energy and, when we begin to access the vibration of each Ray, many changes can occur in our lives.

Working with the Rays and utilizing their energies can open us up to new levels of spirituality, allowing us to progress beyond the confines of our Earth-bound five physical senses to those of clairaudience, intuition, telepathy, clairvoyance, and connection with the Cosmos.

Each Ray manifests its own color in the physical world, but each also has a color on the spiritual plane for those who can "see" color, so they sometimes appear differently. Color is an important ingredient in God's creation, so being able to use the Rays is a key element in our spiritual evolution. Rays can help contribute to knowledge about ourselves and our part in the Cosmos.

The traditional Ray system includes seven Rays, each with its own defining energy and vibrational classification, although people have written of systems with many more classifications. However, I recommend starting with the basic seven Rays, which are the core power of the system. Each Ray has an Archangel, who is responsible for it and who connects with it on a vibrational level.

Angel and a rainbow

These Archangels are called the "Archangels of the Rays." We can call upon the Archangels of the Rays to help us personally and for planetary service.

The following list gives you the qualities of each Ray, together with the crystals and metals that can help strengthen the Ray force when you meditate and open yourself up to your Angels. Using your sense of smell can also enhance the energies derived from the Rays. Sometimes, when working with the Archangels of the Rays, a fragrance can suddenly permeate the air around you. I have listed the fragrances that carry the same vibrational levels as the Rays.

Working with the seven Rays provides a very powerful connection with the Archangels.

Ray 1 • The Blue Ray

Archangel Michael's Ray of Protection and Power

Other Main Properties
Love, Faith, Motivation, Strength, Calm, Transformation, Harmony, and Courage

Associated Crystals
Blue Kunzite, Blue Topaz, Lapis Lazuli

Associated Fragrances
Cedar, Frankincense, Geranium, Myrrh, Palma Rosa, Sage, Tea-Tree

Archangel Michael's attunement to the Ray of Protection and Power is that of the strength of a powerful warrior combined with a love and tenderness that can fill your entire Being. Connection with this Ray can help you to heal and purify your physical body, allowing you to develop your feelings of humility, peace, love, serenity, and spirituality, thus changing your outlook and attitude to the world around you.

Ray 2 • The Yellow Ray

Archangel Jophiel's Ray of Illumination and Wisdom

Other Main Properties
Optimism, Joy, Fun, and Knowledge

Associated Crystals
Citrine, Yellow Sapphire, Yellow Topaz and Amber

Associated Fragrances
Cinnamon, Clove, Pine, Sandalwood

Archangel Jophiel's attunement to the Ray of Illumination and Wisdom brings the gifts of love, light, and warmth to your entire Being, permeating every cell. This will help you to connect with your soul, which in turn will strengthen your communication with your spiritual guides and your Angels. Through utilizing the strength of this Ray you can learn to appreciate the beauty within others and to cherish the wonders of life.

Ray 3 • The Pink Ray

Archangel Chamuel's Ray of Love and Relationships

Other Main Properties
Hope, Intuition, Gratitude, Tolerance, and Compassion

Associated Crystals
Pink Kunzite, Pink Tourmaline, Rose Quartz, and the metal Silver

Associated Fragrances
Jasmine, Gardenia, Hyacinth, Rose Otto, Ylang-Ylang

Archangel Chamuel's attunement to the Ray of Love and Relationships carries a gentle, flowing energy, which brings warmth to your heart, body, and soul. It will open up your heart to develop healing gifts and will attract to you like-minded soul mates. It can also help to repair strained friendships and enhance your relationships. The focus of this Ray will help you to appreciate life and the world around you. It will encourage you to value your "uniqueness" and to develop and use your talents.

Ray 4 • The White Ray

Archangel Gabriel's Ray of Harmony and Purity

Other Main Properties
Understanding, Clarity, Creativeness, Grace, and Purity

Associated Crystals
Clear White Quartz, Diamond, White Sapphire

Associated Fragrances
Basil, Bay, Clary Sage, Nag Champa, Neroli, Rose

Archangel Gabriel's attunement to the Ray of Harmony and Purity is the loving powerful energy of the White Ray, which contains and reflects all colors, merging them to form a brilliant white that will help bring accelerated and unprecedented spiritual growth and enlightenment. This Ray will also help you to realize and understand your true potential and to accomplish what is necessary in order to achieve your goals in life.

Ray 5 • The Green Ray

Archangel Raphael's Ray of Healing

Other Main Properties
Humility, Flawlessness, Communication, Intellect, and Adaptability

Associated Crystals
Emerald, Green Peridot, Green Tourmaline, Moldavite

Associated Fragrances
Mint, Pine, Wintergreen, Sage

Archangel Raphael's attunement to the Green Ray of Healing encompasses a powerful loving energy, which combines green, the color of nature, with that of the radiant power of the Sun to create vitality, truth, beauty, and healing. It will invite harmony into your life to promote personal growth and will help keep physical, mental, and emotional energy balanced. It will enhance creative visualization, divine visions, and intuition, enabling you to focus and seek the truth in all that you do.

Ray 6 • The Gold Ray

Archangel Uriel's Ray of Compassion and Peace

Other Main Properties
Serenity, Honesty, Confidence, Courage, and Justice

Associated Crystals
Rutile Quartz and the metals Yellow and White Gold

Associated Fragrances
Cinnamon, Chamomile, Ginger, Neroli

Archangel Uriel's attunement to the Ray of Compassion is one that is peaceful, graceful, and full of a love that can fill every part of your Being with its energy. Its main focus is to encourage the development and use of spiritual knowledge and energy in order to serve both God and man. Many see flecks of other colors in this Ray—normally ruby and/or deep purple—so sometimes it is called the Ruby Ray or the Ruby-Gold Ray. When you start to work with the Archangel Uriel and this Ray, I suggest that you visualize the color gold and wait to see if this changes to one of the other colors, or if colored specs of ruby and/or purple appear.

Ray 7 • The Violet Ray

Archangel Zadkiel's Ray of Purification and Spiritual Growth

Other Main Properties
Joy, Calm, Mercy, Forgiveness, Transformation, and Grace

Associated Crystal
Amethyst

Associated Fragrances
Lavender and Lilac

Archangel Zadkiel's attunement to the Ray of Purification and Spiritual Growth is a purifying and calming energy, which combines with the love of the Universe to enter your heart and the very essence of your Being— your soul. The energy of this Ray not only focuses on forgiveness, purification, and grace, but its powerful vibrations will help you learn how to open yourself up to become a channel with the Angelic realms.

Meditation to Connect you with the Archangels of the Rays

1 *Take yourself to a quiet place or your sacred space (see page 80), sit in a comfortable chair, remove your shoes, and place the soles of your feet on the floor. Relax and close your eyes.*

2 *Concentrate on your breathing. Breathe in for a count of four through your nose, then out for a count of four through your mouth.*

3 *Visualize the soles of your feet growing strong roots, which descend down through the floor into the soil below. As you breathe in, imagine these roots penetrating deeper and deeper until you are securely anchored to the Earth.*

As you inhale, feel the energies of the Earth draw up into your body via these roots until they fill your whole body.

4 *Now invoke Archangel Michael to fill both your aura and physical body with his Blue Ray. Visualize his Blue Ray entering through the crown of your head to spread around the whole of your body, expanding to fill your aura.*

Ask him to fill you with strength and courage. Ask him to draw his sword and cut any cords and attachments that are binding you to negative thoughts and deeds. Be open to his energy and his words. When you feel this process is complete, thank him and move on.

5 *Now invoke the Archangel Jophiel to pour the Yellow Ray through the crown of your head to fill your mind with the knowledge and wisdom that you have learned since childhood.*

Ask him to help your knowledge and wisdom grow so you can teach and help others. Be open to his energy and his words. When you feel that this process is complete, thank him and move on.

6 *Now open your heart to the Pink Ray of the Archangel Chamuel and visualize it penetrating your physical body as it enters your heart. Invoke him to help you find love, compassion, and the strength to forgive those who may have hurt you in any way.*

Ask him also to forgive you for any hurt you may have caused others, either knowingly or unknowingly. Pause for a time to allow the Archangel Chamuel to complete this, being open to his energies and his words. Thank him, then move on.

7 *Now feel the Archangel Gabriel pour the pure White Ray of Harmony and Purity through the crown of your head, filling your physical self and your aura.*

Ask him for clarity in understanding the lessons you should be learning in this lifetime and to help you clear any blockages holding you back. Ask him to fill your life with joy and generosity to others. Wait for the Archangel Gabriel to do his work and be open to any messages he may have for you. Thank him, then move on.

8 *Next is the Green Ray of the Archangel Raphael. Visualize him pouring his Ray of Healing and Abundance into your physical body, through the crown of your head. If you are ill, ask him to help you; if you know others who are ill ask him to send his Green Ray to help them and also to help the planet. Be open to any communication from the Archangel Raphael, then thank him and move on.*

9 *Now invoke the Archangel Uriel to fill your aura and mind with his Gold Ray of Peace and Serenity. Ask him to help you send out this feeling to others you know and those who may be going through particular difficulties. When you have done this, pause so the Archangel Uriel can complete his work.*
Be open to his energies and his words.
Thank him, then move on.

10 *The last of the seven Archangels to invoke is the Archangel Zadkiel of the Violet Ray. Visualize him pouring this Ray through your crown so that it spreads through your physical body and fills your aura.*

Ask the Archangel Zadkiel to dissolve your feelings of negativity and replace them with joy, happiness, and a love of life. Allow the Archangel Zadkiel to do his work, then be open to any communication he may have for you. Thank him.

You are now filled with the power and energy of the Archangels. Take your time to enjoy their love and feel their protection and healing energy.

11 *When you are ready you will need to close down your spiritual centers of Heavenly communication. Concentrate on your breathing and feel any spiritual energy left within you rise through your body and up through the crown of your head. Visualize it flowing back to the Cosmos, then visualize the top of your head, closing the portal through which the energy entered your body. Visualize the energy of the Earth melting out of your entire being slowly, traveling back down through the roots into the ground. Take your time, open your eyes, become aware of your physical body, and feel renewed.*

Oriental Angel

Working with Individual Archangels of the Rays

You may prefer to focus on working with a specific Archangel, through the energy of his associated Ray and its particular attributes. I suggest that you do at least one of the following in preparation:

1 Light a candle in the associated color of the Archangel and have other articles around you, such as the relevant crystals, jewelry, flowers, or something with the related fragrance. You might wear an article of clothing in the Archangel's color.

2 Relax and concentrate on your breathing. Breathe in for a count of four through your nose, then breathe out for a count of four through your mouth.

3 When you are feeling fully relaxed, place your feet flat on the ground and visualize strong roots growing from the soles of your feet, through the soil, grounding you securely to the Earth.

4 Now visualize strongly the color of the particular Ray you want to work with. As you breathe in, visualize the color you are working with entering your body through your nose with every breath.

5 Relax and feel the colored energy working as it fills your body.

6 Now invoke the associated Archangel to fill the air around you with the color.

7 Take as long as you want to communicate your messages to the Archangel, all the while bathing in the color of his Ray.

8 When you feel ready to finish, change the color of the energy you are breathing in to pure white. Remember to thank the Archangel.

9 Once you feel that the Angelic energy has left your vicinity, allow the roots that descended from the soles of your feet to dissolve back to their original place.

10 When you are ready, open your eyes.

Detail from the **Coronation of the Virgin,** *Sandro Botticelli, tempera on panel, Uffizi Gallery, Florence, Italy. The Bridgeman Art Library.*

Connecting to our Higher Self and the Cosmos through Angels

THE CHAKRAS

Our knowledge of the Chakra system comes from the study of ancient Indian texts. In Sanskrit "chakra" means "wheel" and those who can see them describe the Chakra points as spinning wheels of light. There are seven major Chakra points used in meditation, which are all interrelated. If one Chakra point becomes disturbed or blocked it can upset the functioning of the others—this can manifest itself as an emotional feeling of being depressed, with negativity blocking spiritual attunement and growth. If this blockage remains in place physical problems can develop, stemming from whichever area is most vulnerable.

Developing and Working with Your Chakras

When we begin working with our Chakras, we are searching to raise our spiritual vibrational level. On this first level we are working at what is known as the third-dimensional frequency. It is via this frequency that we are connected with our Higher Self— our soul—our physical body's counterpart in the Cosmos. Each Chakra has a different function and vibrates at a different frequency. The vibration of the color associated with each Chakra is an important ingredient in the way it works to connect your physical body with the Cosmos. When working with the third-dimensional Chakras to help your spiritual development, using crystals can enhance your connection—the vibrational energy of the crystal's color working with the colors of the Chakras adds extra power. The best way to work with crystals is to lie on the floor and lay the specific crystal on the Chakra point. If using crystals, please note that clear quartz can be substituted for any of the others mentioned.

Learning to use the third-dimensional Chakras can be the first part of your journey to open yourself up to the Angelic realms, and to working with Angels and spiritual guides. There are specific Archangels in charge of helping the development of each Chakra, with the Archangel Gabriel in charge of the first two.

First or Base Chakra
Archangel Gabriel

Location Base of Spine
Function Grounding
Associated Color Red
Associated Crystals Red Jasper,
Red Tiger's Eye
Related Physical Areas Large intestine,
adrenal system, rectum, muscles, lower
back, legs and feet

This Chakra grounds us in our physical
existence on Earth. Its energy helps us to
blend the physical practicalities of our life
with the spiritual. It gives us the energy
to make a success of our life, work, and
relationships and will eliminate that which
is no longer needed for growth. If it is
unbalanced, we may suffer depression,
be afraid of life, and become selfish
and self-centered.

Second or Sacral Chakra
Archangel Gabriel

Location Lower abdomen just above
the pelvic bone
Function Sexuality
Associated Color Orange
Associated Crystal Carnelian
Related Physical Areas Lower intestine,
kidneys, reproductive organs, hormones,
bladder, bowels, bronchitis, asthma, blood
circulatory system

This Chakra is directly related to the energies
of the five physical senses, plus creativity
and sexuality. When working correctly it
gives you energy and the feeling of being
fully alive and has the spontaneous effect
of removing fear of the unknown.

Third or Solar Plexus Chakra
Archangel Jophiel

Location Navel and solar plexus area
Function Personal power
Associated Color Yellow
Associated Crystals Citrine, Amber or Yellow
Tiger's Eye
Related Physical Areas Digestive system,
liver, gall bladder, spleen

This Chakra encourages physical and
material power, helping you to master the
physical world—especially helping you to
achieve your hopes and dreams. It helps and
encourages you to express your individuality
and stand out from the crowd. When
functioning normally it will booster your
self-confidence and enable you to achieve
a true sense of self-awareness, which will
encourage you to pursue your dreams. If this
Chakra is unbalanced the opposite happens;
you feel insecure and lack self-confidence
and may become aggressive and a bully.

Fourth or Heart Chakra
Archangel Raphael

Location Heart
Function Love and healing
Associated Color Green
Associated Crystals Aventurine, Amazonite,
Malachite, Emerald, Peridot
Related Physical Areas Heart conditions,
thymus gland, immune system, headaches,
migraine, and related symptoms of stress

This Chakra is the center of our emotional
well-being and encourages us to give
unconditional love to those around us.
At the same time it encourages people to
return this abundance of love. When it is
blocked we feel unloved, which can lead
to depression.

Fifth or Throat Chakra
Archangel Michael

Location Throat
Function Communication
Associated Color Blue
Associated Crystals Sodalite, Blue Howlite
Related Physical Areas Thyroid system, weight and its associated problems, teeth and gums

This Chakra controls mental creativity and communication. When it is balanced we can easily communicate with others, both verbally and in writing. When it is blocked it can lead to communication difficulties and you may not be able to convey what you mean to others. Also, because of its position, if this Chakra is not being put to good use communicating it seems to turn its energies to excessive drinking and eating instead, causing weight problems.

Sixth or Third Eye Chakra
Archangel Raziel

Location Between the eyebrows
Function Inner wisdom, intuition
Associated Color Indigo
Associated Crystal Lapis Lazuli
Related Physical Areas Head, eyes, ears, nose, pituitary gland, and headaches

This area is where our "sixth" sense manifests itself. When unblocked, it is the source of intuition, ESP, clairvoyance, and all other psychic abilities. When blocked, it can lead to irrational thoughts, insomnia, and anxiety.

Seventh or Crown Chakra
Archangel Zadkiel

Location Crown of the head
Function Spiritual understanding
Associated Color Violet
Associated Crystal Amethyst
Related Physical Areas Immune system,
relieves pain and helps the physical healing
process

It is through this Chakra that we can become
a clear channel to the Cosmos and thus to
the Angelic realms. When it is in balance,
we can understand our life's purpose and
realize how we are connected to all forms of
life. When it is blocked, we can be left with
a feeling of overwhelming loneliness.

Angel Gabriel, *Simone Martini, 14th century, tempera and gold leaf on panel, Koninktyk Museum voor Schone Kunsten, Antwerp, Belgium. Giraudon/The Bridgeman Art Library.*

Meditation to Open and Unblock Your Third-Dimensional Chakras

1 *Take yourself to a quiet place where you will not be disturbed, or to your sacred space (see page 80). Sit in a comfortable chair, take off your shoes, and relax. Close your eyes.*

2 *Concentrate on your breathing. Breath in through your nose to a count of four, then expel through your mouth to a count of four. Now imagine that the soles of your feet have roots that are growing downward, through the floor, down, down, through any structures beneath you, down until they reach the ground. With every breath you take these roots are burrowing deeper and deeper into the Earth.*

3 *Once they have gone as deep as they can, imagine that with every in-breath you are inhaling the energy of the Universe up through the roots into your body, filling your physical self. With every out-breath, you are banishing tensions and toxins from your body. Feel the energy of the Universe draw up from the roots, up into the soles of your feet, through to the Base Chakra at the base of your spine. Visualize a red lotus flower growing here then invoke the name of the Archangel Gabriel, asking him to enter your body and help open up this beautiful flower. Visualize a Ray of light pinpointing this part of your body and see the flower's petals opening*

as you inhale. Feel this Chakra point unblock, and sense the feelings of belonging, of being you and feeling wonderful.

4 Now feel this flow of energy continue up to the second chakra, just above the pubic bone, and visualize the orange lotus flower situated here. Invoke the Archangel Gabriel to help you release the energy stored here. As the flower opens, bathe in the feelings of creativity that will overcome you and become aware of the wonderful person you are.

5 When you are ready, let the energy move upward to the Third Chakra situated within your Solar Plexus. Invoke the Archangel Jophiel and visualize a Ray of yellow light opening up the petals of the yellow lotus flower positioned at this point. As this happens, be aware that this is the point in your body where you will be able to pick up the feelings of others and once it is opened you will be able to feel both the happiness and sorrow of the world. Ask Jophiel for guidance and to teach you how to control being open to these feelings.

6 Now feel the flow of energy quicken as it travels upward to reach the Heart Chakra. Invoke the Archangel Raphael as you visualize a Ray of green light to open up the green lotus flower sited here. As you breathe in and out feel the two-way flow of love that you are giving and receiving, both to your Angelic helpers and also to the collective human consciousness.

7 When you are ready, continue the flow of energy until it reaches the center of your throat. Call upon the Archangel Michael to send out his blue Ray of light to open up the blue lotus flower here, so your communication skills can develop and flow freely. Ask him to help you to learn the gift of truly listening to those people around you, as well as to your Angelic helpers.

8 As you open and unblock your Chakras, the energy within you will grow and gather strength. Now let it move upward to the point at the center of your forehead known as the Sixth Chakra or the Third Eye. Call upon the Archangel Raziel to pierce this point with indigo Rays of color and imagine the indigo lotus flower opening its precious petals. This center of extrasensory awareness will open up to let you see beyond the boundaries of the five senses of the physical world.

9 When you are ready, allow the energy flow to travel to the top of your head, to the Crown Chakra. Invoke the Archangel Zadkiel to send his Ray of violet to open up and unblock this Chakra and imagine a beautiful violet lotus flower unfolding its petals. As it does so, visualize the energy it contains sending a violet light radiating up through the crown of your head, up through to the Cosmos, so you become an open channel to the Angelic and spiritual realms.

10 *Feel the energy flowing from this point upward. Now visualize all the colors of your Chakra system flowing freely upward with the Ray of violet, so that you become a two-way channel between your physical body and your Higher Self. You are a rainbow of living light, connected to the Universe and to your Angels—but simultaneously connected and grounded to the Earth.*

11 *Be aware of the energy pulsating through you. Thank your Angels for helping you to take this step, so you can shake off the shackles that have bound you to a physical existence and become aware of the spiritual world. When you are ready, it is very important to "close" yourself down correctly. Failure to do this can mean you are open and party to the innermost feelings of people you come into contact with.*

12 *First, shut down the Ray of energy emanating from the crown of your head, breaking off your connection with the Universe.*
   Concentrate on your breathing and feel the Ray of violet shut down gradually, allowing the violet lotus flower to close its petals. Now feel the energy descend through your body, making sure that you visualize the lotus flower at each Chakra point closing its petals completely.

13 *Feel the energy of the Earth empty out of you, through the roots growing from the soles of your feet, back down into the Earth. Now feel the roots growing out of the soles of your feet come back up into your body. Remember to thank your Angels for helping you to do this very powerful meditation. When you are ready, open your eyes, feel your limbs, and become aware of where you are.*

As you start to work with your Chakras, you will raise your spiritual consciousness. The way your mind works and the way you see the world around you will change. Your mind will no longer be restricted to using just the five senses—you have grown beyond their limitations. For many, it also opens up communication with spiritual healers who wish to continue helping those still on Earth. Those who have followed this path are often called "light workers" and they are aware that they have been put on this Earth with a higher spiritual purpose. More and more people are becoming aware of their higher consciousness and taking steps to tune into it to help their fellow man.

ANGELS AND WORKING WITH CANDLES

Working with different colored candles is a way of focusing your mind on specific intentions or on communication with the Angelic realms. There are a number of different ways to utilize the power of colored candles when working with your Angels; use the method that you feel most comfortable and relaxed with.

Preparing and Using the Candles

Before you begin, you may wish to dedicate your candle specifically to your Angelic communication. Hold your candle in both hands and concentrate as you ask a particular Archangel, or your Angels in general, to come through for you, using words that feel right. An example of what you might say is:

I dedicate this (state color) candle to you and invite you to come into my life. Let your love and harmony surround me. I open up my heart and soul to you and welcome you.

When burning a candle for this purpose you may wish to let it burn through until it is finished—in which case it is very important not to leave it unattended as it could be a fire hazard. Alternatively, you may prefer to blow the candle out once you have finished

your meditations, as this can help to give a feeling of closure. If you are using your candle for only a short period, you may wish to use it again later for the same purpose. Once it is finished and cooled down, either leave it in its holder—as long as no one will touch it—or wrap it up to keep it protected until you want to use it again.

Candles and the Archangels of the Rays

If you wish to communicate specifically with the different Archangels of the Rays it is beneficial to use candles of a related color, to help focus your mind.

Blue Archangel Michael for protection, strength, and courage

Yellow Archangel Jophiel for wisdom and knowledge

Pink Archangel Chamuel for love and compassion

White Archangel Gabriel for harmony, understanding, clarity and purity

A blue candle symbolizes Archangel Michael.

Green Archangel Raphael for healing

Gold Archangel Uriel for peace and serenity

Violet Archangel Zadkiel for joy and mercy

Invoking Your Archangel Before lighting your candles, relax. Dedicate the use of the candle to a specific Archangel by saying something like this:

I invite you, Archangel (name of angel) to enter my life. I dedicate this (color of candle) to you. I welcome you with all my heart. Please enlighten me with your wisdom and love.

When you are finished remember to thank your Archangel.

Archangel Raphael is associated with healing and the color green.

Burn a violet candle for Archangel Zadkiel.

Working with all the Angels

Another method I find very successful is to use colors that are specific to a particular purpose, which allows you to be open to any Angel who is waiting to assist and communicate with you. The following chart is for guidance, so if you feel you would like to substitute a different color it really is not a problem. The candles are a tool to help you focus your mind and to help raise your vibrational levels, so that you can become an open channel with the Cosmos. Working this way will help you communicate with the different Angels who are waiting for you to invite them into your life, so they can help and guide you in different ways.

White can replace all other colors. It also helps you to focus on spirituality, peace, tranquility, harmony, clairvoyance, meditation, inner peace, and truth.

Red can symbolize energy, strength, courage, vitality, and willpower. It can also stimulate sexual passion, lust, and virility.

Pink is associated with love, both romantic and platonic. It also encourages affection, friendship, romance, success, kindness, gentleness, and willpower.

Purple is associated with the development of psychic and spiritual abilities, and generally with spiritual growth. It symbolizes power, ambition, material wealth, wisdom, and healing.

Black can help remove negative energy by absorbing it, therefore protecting you. If you are alone it can help you feel safe.

Silver can help you focus on the gifts of clairvoyance, inspiration, intuition, dreams, higher wisdom, intellect, purity, compassion, and inner stability.

Gold attracts positive influences and happiness and is very helpful in matters of your career. It also encourages inner confidence, understanding, memory, concentration, creativity, imagination, and knowledge.

Yellow can help to enhance your confidence and intellect and improve your memory. Spiritually it will help you to raise your visualization abilities. Yellow also encourages happiness, vitality, attraction, and charm.

Green is the color of luck, good fortune, money, and prosperity, although remember that financial gain must be in balance and not lead to greed. It is also the color of spiritual healing.

Orange is for career and business/monetary matters and is perfect for helping to bring legal matters to a conclusion. Its energy also enhances courage, study, intellect, knowledge, creativity, and understanding.

Blue can help you center on higher wisdom, inner peace, inspiration, intuition, dreams, truth, and understanding.

Never leave burning candles unattended.

Meditation for Using Candles

1 *Choose the candle either to represent the Archangel you wish to call upon, or for the desired purpose.*

2 *Take yourself to a quiet place, your sacred space or Angelic altar (see page 80). You can enhance the energy of candles by also using crystals of the same color. Clear Quartz can replace any color, or it can be added to the crystals you are using to amplify their vibrations.*

3 *Light your candle and place in a safe holder, take off your shoes, sit comfortably, and watch the candle flame.*

4 *Now begin your breathing exercise. Breathe in through your nose for a count of four, then breathe out through your mouth for a count of four.*

5 *When you are ready, visualize roots growing downward through the Earth from the soles of your feet.*

6 *Either invoke the name of the Archangel you wish to work with, or open yourself up to the Angelic realms in general by invoking your Angels to communicate with you. If you are using the second method, think about why you have chosen a particular color of candle. Meditate and contemplate why you have*
called upon your Angels. Take your time doing this and enjoy the peace and harmony you will be feeling.

7 *When you feel that you are finished, thank your Angels and concentrate on your breathing again.*
Visualize the roots that grew from the soles of your feet shrinking back gradually into your body. Take some time to sit quietly before getting up.

Blow out your candle—or, if you are going to let it burn down naturally, make sure it is not left unattended.

WORKING WITH CRYSTALS

Crystals have been treasured for both their beauty and their energy since the dawn of civilization. They are part of the heritage of humankind, having been formed within the bowels of Mother Earth, never losing their color and brilliance. Priests, shamans, spiritual seekers, and healers have used them for thousands of years.

Each crystal exhibits its own individual pulse of energy. An example of this can be seen in watches with a Quartz crystal movement—they keep time accurately via the pulse in the crystal. This energy can help us enhance and amplify the strength of the communications our Angels are sending us, very much like using a megaphone. The energies found within the world of minerals are a gift from the Cosmos, so when you access and use these energies you are connecting with a tool that has been made available to help us connect with the Universe.

Many of you reading this book may have already reached a point where you are consciously seeking to raise your level of knowledge about your Higher Self and also about the Angelic and spiritual realms. Crystals have physical form and structure that link us to the physical world around us, but they also have particular energies that can help our spiritual journey. Every crystalline structure is individual, with its own color, form, and energy. Each can be used in a distinctive way, not only to understand the nature of our existence on this planet but also to help us explore the heavenly realms.

Choosing Your Crystals

There are a number of ways to choose crystals. You may look at the many selections available that list their properties, and decide that this is the basis on which you would like to work with them. Some people prefer to dowse for their crystal with a pendulum, or simply pass their hand over a selection to see if they can feel a slight vibration. Another way is to look at a selection of crystals and just go with your gut feeling, choosing the one that appeals to you most. There is a saying that you do not choose the crystal—it chooses you. A number of years ago I had shops selling crystals to the public and I noticed that if someone came in for a crystal and was just looking randomly, they normally bought the first crystal that they had picked up—even if they looked at others afterward.

The seven Chakras and associated crystals by color: Base Chakra (Red Jasper), Sacral Chakra (Carnelian), Solar Plexus (Citrine), Heart (Malachite), Throat (Blue Lace Agate), Third Eye (Purple Fluorite), and Crown (Amethyst).

When buying crystals, keep in mind that some crystals may have been dyed, and it is always better to try to buy natural crystal. I have found that you particularly need to double-check Citrine, since it is often dyed. You also need to check that Turquoise is not dyed Howlite—if it is, it will have the healing properties of Howlite, not Turquoise.

Cleansing Your Crystals

It is important to cleanse your crystals properly because crystals retain the memory of everyone that has touched them, so you need to wipe this memory clean. Ideally they should be washed in the sea or natural running water, but in our modern world this is normally not possible.

I always suggest soaking them in water containing sea salt, or washing them under a running faucet instead. Some people bury their crystals in their garden to cleanse them —if you do this, make sure you mark the place so that you can find them again! Another way to cleanse them is to use a smudge stick, allowing its smoke to surround the crystals.

A number of fragile crystals, such as Moldavite, should not be put in salt water.

Programming Your Crystals

Once your crystals are cleansed, you must program them. This is to instruct their energies as to how you want to use them— perhaps for attunement or transformation. The most practical way to do this is to hold the crystal in your hand and affirm inwardly the purpose for which it will be used—perhaps for healing, love, or meditation.

Crystals empowered by Angelic energy

Alternatively you can devise a precise affirmation that will accurately describe the purpose of the programming—for instance, to be an open channel with the Angelic realms.

Or you may do a simple meditation while holding your crystal, asking for the Angels to energize it with their love and light.

Do not let other people touch your crystals once they have been cleansed and programmed,

because the crystals will pick up and store their vibrations and energies.

Using Crystals

If you are right-handed, hold your crystal in your left hand—vice versa if you are left handed. With practice, you will be able to feel the subtle electric currents contained within the crystal. There are a number of ways in which to work with your crystals—the best thing, as always, is to go with the flow and work however you feel most comfortable.

Working with Crystals Dedicated to the Angelic Realms

Here are some of the crystals that I personally enjoy working with, along with their reputed properties. When working with the Archangels of the Rays there are particular crystals that align with the energy of the specific Rays, and I have listed these for you on pages 118–21. However, these are only suggestions. If you are drawn intuitively to other crystals then those will be the best ones for you to use.

Amber This is actually a fossilized tree resin, not a crystal. Amber can help you connect your conscious mind to the spiritual realms. It is said to contain the memory of the planet and can be a powerful aid in helping you with your own intellect and memory. It brings the energies of protection, psychic shielding, sensuality, balance, and calmness to those who wear it. It can help cleanse its environment by drawing out negativity and is said to be particularly useful in purifying

Amber

maternity delivery rooms. It can also purify mental, emotional, and spiritual minds when it is worn or carried. Its vibrational levels are associated with the Yellow Ray of the Archangel Jophiel.

Reputed Physical Healing Attributes

Disorders of the kidneys, bladder, lungs, heart, bones, digestive tract, and throat. It is excellent for general healing purposes.

Amethyst This is the stone of spirituality and can help transform your third-dimensional energies, which keep you anchored to your physical existence on Earth, into the higher frequencies of the spiritual and Angelic realms. It does this by balancing, stabilizing, and cleansing your emotional, mental, and physical bodies, together with your auric body. It can help you to know and understand the perfect peace that you experienced before your birth on this planet. It contains

Amethyst

the very high vibration found within the Violet Ray of the Archangel Zadkiel, which can help you find mercy and joy and open you up to communication with all the Heavenly realms. It is a very powerful healing crystal and can amplify absent healing. It is thought that it can protect against psychic attack, the vibrations contained within the Amethyst transforming the negative energy of an attack into a positive loving energy, which is then conveyed to the Cosmos.

Reputed Physical Healing Attributes

Disorders of hearing, skeletal system, nervous system, digestive tract, stomach, teeth and heart. It is also used in the treatment of insomnia and arthritis. It is said to help with pain relief and to alleviate headaches and migraines—people often keep a few Amethyst crystals in their fridge to place on their temples when required. In ancient Rome Amethyst would be crushed and added to wine in order to prevent drunkenness. Today it is said to assist with healing alcoholism, compulsive behaviour and all kinds of addictions.

Angel Aura

Ametrine A natural mix of Amethyst and Citrine, containing all the properties associated with both crystals. It can help enhance the link between your physical self and your psychic self and using it can arouse your intellect to reach beyond the five physical senses, intensifying their link with the unconscious mind and onward to the soul. This will enable you to reach and enter the gateway through which we need to travel to communicate with the Cosmos. When used with meditation and attunement, Ametrine will accelerate your progress to the higher states of consciousness, speeding up your communicational skills and dialogue with your Angels—and, for those working with them, our spiritual guides.

Reputed Physical Healing Attributes Useful in helping us recognize changes to our body during periods of growth and during periods of change, such as pregnancy or the menopause. It also has the healing attributes of both Amethyst and Citrine.

Angel Aura Quartz Also sometimes called Opal Aura, Rainbow Aura, or Pearl Aura, this is a quartz that has been scientifically treated by fusing platinum and/or silver crystals with heat in a vacuum, which gives this crystal its striking Angelic coloring. The iridescent colors, together with this crystal's high spiritual energy, can quickly and powerfully help you attune to communication with the Angelic realms. When used with

Angelite

meditation, it can also help connect you with your Higher Self and your inner wisdom, by awakening and accelerating your spiritual awareness. It can also help you to find and understand your purpose in life, as well as heightening awareness of Angelic protection, helping you to feel peace and tranquility.

Reputed Physical Healing Attributes Angel Aura is helpful for general health and vitality. It is also said to help with the healing process of all illnesses, including those that have not responded well to other treatments, orthodox or complementary.

Angelite This quartz is blue and white, but occasionally contains small amounts of red hematite. It was discovered in Peru in South America in 1987, around the time of the Harmonic Convergence—an organized New Age spiritual gathering, which took place on August 16–17, 1987. Groups of people gathered at numerous sacred sites around

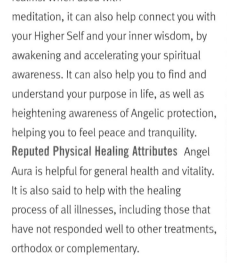

the world to welcome in a new era of spiritual development— the date was based on the ancient Mayan calendar and on interpretations of different forms of astrology. As its name suggests, Angelite is an excellent stone to help you to work with the Angelic realms and its vibrational levels will help your attunement and connection with all the Heavenly realms. It raises your states of conscious and spiritual awareness, helping you to understand, focus, and connect with the Cosmos, and can help clear you spiritually so you can become an open channel with your Angels and with spiritual guides, giving you guidance with healing.

It can also help heal anger, encouraging forgiveness and promoting inner calm and peace. It is believed to be very helpful in telepathic communication, acting as both a receiver and a sender; if two people wish to be connected they should carry a piece of Angelite programmed for this purpose. The powerful communication energy means Angelite can help us heal our relationships with others, allowing us to interact on many different levels. It can help us stop blaming ourselves or others when things go wrong,

Aquamarine

by promoting harmony within ourselves and in our outward attitudes, helping us tune into feelings of connection with all living things.

Reputed Physical Healing Attributes

Angelite is said to help in the treatment of infectious disease, headaches, throat inflammations and infections, heart function, and the circulatory system. It can also help lower blood pressure and balance an overactive thyroid.

Aquamarine Aquamarine is an excellent stone to help you adjust and feel comfortable with higher levels of spiritual awareness. It imparts mental and emotional stability and enhances the link with your Higher Self. Using this crystal when working with your Angels will give you a good grounding and feeling of security, while your spiritual awareness, feelings, and energies soar to new and previously unfelt levels.

Reputed Physical Healing Attributes

Aquamarine has been used in the treatment of swollen glands and is said to be successful in stimulating the glands. It assists in looking after the teeth and is good for the eyes, improving vision.

Black Tourmaline This crystal, which to many is quite unattractive, is a very powerful crystal of protection, repelling and absorbing negative energies for individuals or within the environment. It is often used as an aura cleanser and can help you to attain higher levels of spiritual awareness. Because of this, it is essential to wash this crystal more often than others because it can get overloaded with energies and stop working. It can also help to dispel fears, obsessions, and neuroses, increasing your emotional stability and intellect, and help increase your physical vigor.

Reputed Physical Healing Attributes It is particularly beneficial in the treatment of arthritis, heart disease, and any problems with the adrenal glands. It can help those with dyslexia, help people with anxiety to feel calmer, and also strengthen the immune system.

Citrine

Celestite Celestite comes in many colors and forms, including white, blue, orange, red, and yellow. In general it is excellent for mental agility, helping you to understand complex problems. It can also help those who suffer from emotional pain, fear, anxiety, and negative thinking, by overcoming them with relaxation, calmness, inner peace, and love. Blue Celestite, which is often bought in geode form, is particularly powerful in helping to focus communication with the Angelic realms; it is said that it was given powers by the Angels to raise consciousness and to help us to connect with them.

Reputed Physical Healing Attributes

Celestite helps with digestive problems, eye problems, mental disorders, eliminating toxins, and hearing.

Citrine When buying Citrine, always try to make sure that it is natural because there are many dyed varieties on sale. This crystal does not accumulate negative energy, so it does not normally need cleansing. It is known as a "merchant's stone" because it is said to help merchants run a successful business and not only acquire wealth but maintain that wealth. It stimulates self-

Love, light, peace, and harmony on earth

awareness, wisdom, knowledge, and intuitive skills and also helps align and clear your auric body, so it becomes a pure extension of your physical body. Its properties are aligned with the Yellow Ray of the Archangel Jophiel.

Reputed Physical Healing Attributes Aiding digestive problems, helping to balance the thyroid and working on the circulatory system, liver, gall bladder, and nervous system.

Clear Quartz This is a powerful "all singing, all dancing" crystal, which can be used for all things. Its vibrational properties can amplify,

Putti, detail from **The Sistine Madonna,** *Raphael, 1513, oil on canvas, Gemaeldegaline Alte Meister, Dresden, Germany. Staatliche Kunstsammlungen, Dresden/The Bridgeman Art Library.*

transform, store, and focus energy and it is said to bring the energy of the stars into the soul. It can help align your Earth-bound mental and emotional energies with that of the Universe, helping you to rise above your five senses and making you find and use your sixth sense to accelerate your spiritual growth. In doing this, your mind enters an altered state of consciousness as when you meditate, amplifying and stimulating your psychic and spiritual abilities. This crystal is associated with the White Ray of the Archangel Gabriel and will enhance your mental attributes of clarity, understanding, and calm in all situations. It can help dissipate and heal negative thoughts, helping you replace them with positive thoughts of love, light, peace, and harmony for all humankind and life upon this planet. Quartz can also be used to cleanse, purify, and activate all of the Chakra energy centers of the body.

Reputed Physical Healing Attributes Clear Quartz can help with all forms of healing and can be used in conjunction with all other crystals. It may also help in the treatment of disorders of the digestive system, kidneys, bladder, and circulatory system. It can help to reduce fever and relieve pain.

Emerald The green color of emerald is a sign of spring. Ancient Egyptians believed that emeralds represented rebirth and fertility, and even that the stone could help ease childbirth. Many Egyptian mummies were buried with Emeralds around their necks because an Emerald was believed to endow its wearer with eternal youth. In other times the Emerald was a talisman to ward off evil

spirits and possessions. The Emerald is part of the beryl family and is known as the Stone of Peace. It is a soft and gentle healer, balancing the energies of the spiritual self. Its green energy makes it a perfect stone for alignment with the emerald Green Ray of the Archangel Raphael.

Emerald is a stone of great wisdom and can be used to enhance the memory and to fuel capacity for mental growth and agility. It can also help merge intelligence with sensitivity, wisdom, and judgment, helping you to make the right choice when making decisions. It is also associated with boosting love and fidelity, harmony, growth, patience, inspiration, abundance, and peace. During meditation it will assist you to maintain rhythmic breathing, helping you to sustain your spiritual journal. It is also a powerful aid for the emotional and mental powers of will power, mental clarity, and helping with depression.

Reputed Physical Healing Attributes Emerald is said to help cure insomnia, detoxify the blood, and cure ailments of the heart, eye, pancreas, backbone, lymph notes, intestines, kidneys, and thymus. It is also believed that it can help with the complications of diabetes.

Kunzite Once you get used to holding this crystal, which is normally wand-shaped, you will be amazed how powerful the energy pulse is. This is another crystal that never needs cleansing, because it will not retain negative energy or vibrations. It is great at assisting meditation and is capable of aligning all the Chakras automatically with no conscious direction. It can also help stimulate communication with your Angels. Blue Kunzite will enhance your psychic abilities, channeling, visualization, and meditation, and help you achieve tranquility and serenity. Its energy works well with that of the Archangel Michael and its properties and vibrations are that of the Blue Ray, which will help you to "cut away" any negative mental, emotional, or spiritual attitudes keeping you bound to your past.

Pink Kunzite holds the properties and vibrations of the Pink Ray, so helping your communication with the Archangel Chamuel. It works equally well on mind, body, and spirit and helps encourage self-discipline, promote emotional balance from within ourselves, and attract unconditional love.

Reputed Physical Healing Attributes

Kunzite can help ameliorate stress and panic attacks. Its use can also help remove energy blockages within ourselves, which could later lead to the onset of physical symptoms.

Lapis Lazuli This stone is believed to have existed since time began. It is said to give us the wisdom to understand the mysteries of ancient texts and spiritual ideas, thus giving us access to esoteric planetary knowledge. It is a stone of total awareness, helping you to develop your capacity for wisdom, knowledge, clarity, and inspiration in both a mental and a spiritual way. It can help overcome depression and encourage self-confidence and feelings of serenity and calm. It is often used as a protection against psychic attack or if you feel a victim of the "evil eye"—which is often called "negative energy." The vibration of this stone is associated with the energies of the Blue Ray of the Archangel Michael. Legend has it that an Angel gave this blue stone in a ring to King Solomon —a great crystal wearer—to enable him to control the many demons that he used to build his temple.

Lapis Lazuli

Reputed Physical Healing Attributes Lapis is said to help in the treatment of the throat, bone marrow, and immune system, and with insomnia and vertigo. It is also said to help with high blood pressure and the thyroid gland. However, do not use it regularly if you have low blood pressure.

Moldavite Moldavite is a tektite that was formed over 15 million years ago and can only be found in one area of the world, the Bohemian plateau of the Czech Republic. It is a stone of extra-terrestrial origin, having been formed as a result of a meteorite crash; the pressure and heat of the meteorite impact resulted in this beautiful and powerful crystal. It has a very high vibrational level and is said to stimulate those on this Earth who aspire to reach out to the spiritual and Angelic realms. Its green healing energy is attuned to the healing Green Ray of the Archangel Raphael.

I personally always wear this crystal when I am doing healing, because I feel that it allows easy passage for my spiritual healing helpers to enter the environment I am working in. I also feel it gives me added protection from the emotionally painful debris that can emanate from my patients. I was attracted to Moldavite the first time

Madonna with Angels, *right wing of the* "**Wilton Diptych**": (**Richard II adoring the Madonna**), *French school, c. 1395, on wood, the National Gallery, London, UK. akg-images/Eric Lessing.*

I saw it, long before I knew of its healing energies. This was a number of years before I knew that I would be practicing spiritual healing and working with and channeling my Angels. This is an example of how the crystals you are attracted to are actually choosing you to use their energy!

Reputed Physical Healing Attributes This is a powerful all-round healer, which can assist in raising the vibrational level in all healing. It can also help with fertility issues, hair loss, and promoting the production of new cells. Do not cleanse Moldavite with salt as it is quite fragile.

Moonstone As its name suggests, the energy of this crystal is strongly connected with the cycles of the Moon (see page 112–13). It is a stone for wishing and hoping and can help absorb the spiritual knowledge that you need to help you evolve, rather than the knowledge that you think you want. It is a stone that will help you to expand your intuitive instincts, bringing the possibility of insight and hidden opportunities. It also stimulates confidence, creativity, self-expression, and the gift of the wisdom of diplomacy. It particularly enhances feminine energies, sensitivity, and intuition. This was once called the "traveler's stone" and was used as protection when traveling. It is also often used as an amulet of good fortune.

Reputed Physical Healing Attributes This crystal is said to aid in the treatment of circulatory disorders, adrenal gland problems, insect stings or bites, and

insomnia. It is said to be of particular benefit to women of all ages, helping to enhance fertility or ease the symptoms of PMS and the change of life. It is also said to help with the passage of pregnancy and childbirth.

Obsidian

Obsidian This provides excellent grounding power, which is important when you are aspiring to contact and work with the spiritual and Angelic realms. It is also a powerful protector against negative energy. Wearing obsidian can help to dispel self-inflicted mental and emotional pain, leading to feelings of well-being and the true enjoyment of life. Obsidian carries the energy levels that can ease connection with the Archangel Uriel, helping you to have the gifts of clarity and insight—especially when dealing with others. There are many forms of obsidian so here is a breakdown of a few of the most commonly available types and their reputed qualities:

Apache Tear is said to comfort and soothe in times of deep distress and grief, helping you to have the insight and acceptance that lead you to overcome these times of despair.

This stone can also help to dispel mental blockages and grievances that bind you to the past, allowing you to move forward and learn to forgive both others and yourself. It is also an excellent meditation tool, especially for clarifying issues and gaining insight. It supposedly gets its name from the tears of Apache women grieving for their warriors, who were driven to the edge of a mountain by the cavalry and chose to jump rather than be captured. It is said that if you carry an Apache Tear you will never again shed tears of grief.

Snowflake Obsidian

Reputed Physical Healing Attributes
Apache Tear is said to help muscle spasms and to eliminate toxins from the body.

Snowflake Obsidian enhances well-being and physical health, heightening courage and promoting the enjoyment of life.

Reputed Physical Healing Attributes
Snowflake Obsidian is said to be beneficial in the treatment of bones.

Green Obsidian can help you remove the energies of those around you who have anchored themselves onto your auric body. These people are often called "energy vampires"—they love to suck at your energy because it helps them feel better about themselves. Once they are removed you will feel relief and sometimes a little light-headed. This stone can continue to protect you from these "vampires," directing them to the healing energy of white light, which will give them the help they need.

Reputed Physical Healing Attributes When used by spiritual healers, this crystal can help find and treat the cause of illness. Green Obsidian can also help with problems of the heart and gall bladder.

Rose Quartz The crystal of love attracts both platonic and romantic emotions and relationships, and can bring calm and harmony. It can also help you to appreciate the beauty of art, music, and the written word. A very soothing and comforting stone, its healing energy can help to ease the emotional wounds which you pick up on your life's journey. This can include the stress and tension of life-changing traumatic situations such as bereavement, job loss, divorce, and

break-ups with a loved one. Its gentle and healing properties are attuned to the Pink Ray of the Archangel Chamuel and are great for Angel meditation and channeling.

Reputed Physical Healing Attributes Rose Quartz helps to treat problems of the kidneys and adrenal glands. If you place it upon the Heart Chakra, it can help with easing any stress or pain throughout your body.

Rutile Quartz This crystal is also known as "Angel Hair," because the golden rutile inclusions look like fine hair. It has all the qualities of clear quartz (see pages 148-149), plus the energies of the rutiles. These include strength with love, calm when faced with transition, and the stabilizing of relationships, marriage, and mental thought processes. Rutile quartz can also help to unblock any emotional or physical imbalances hindering your spiritual growth. This crystal has the vibrational energy of the Gold Ray of the Archangel Uriel, bringing you peace and serenity.

Reputed Physical Healing Attributes As well as benefits associated with clear quartz, the rutiles help with allergies and bronchitis.

Sodalite Sodalite enhances self-esteem and helps you to utilize and develop your mental thought processes to arrive at logical conclusions, eliminating confusion and sidetracks. Through this energy it allows you to use your intuitive thoughts to understand and expand your knowledge of the Universe. This is an excellent stone to use in group meditation sessions, focusing feelings of comradeship, friendship, mutual trust, and concentration within the group to help it attain its goals and purpose. Its energies are in tune with those of the Archangel Ariel, who can help you understand how you can help with planetary healing by appreciating all living things.

Reputed Physical Healing Attributes Sodalite is said to help with insomnia and digestive problems, and to ease those disorders associated with calcium deficiency.

Angels of the Mandorla Christi, *a section from* **The Last Judgment,** *Giotto di Bondone, c. 1303–1306, fresco, Arena Chapel, Padua, Italy. agk-images/Cameraphoto.*

Sodalite

Angels & Astrology

The zodiac is divided into 12 astrological signs associated with the 12 known star constellations. Association between the Angels and the astrological signs comes from long-held traditions.

There are many different lists of Angel and astrological associations, but this is the one that I have put together with a little help from my Angels! The link between yourself and your Zodiac Angel is enhanced by the personality traits with which your Zodiac sign has endowed you.

Star Sign Angel Traits

Aries – Chamael (Camuel)
Positive, Assertive

Taurus – Ashmodel
Tenacious, Practical

Gemini – Raguel
Outgoing, Sociable

Cancer – Gabriel
Intuitive, Sensitive

Leo – Michael
Powerful, Courageous

Virgo – Raphael
Methodical, Intellectual

Libra – Jehoel
Mediator, Nurturer

Scorpio – Metatron
Intense, Magnetic

Sagittarius – Zadkiel
Broad-minded, Outgoing

Capricorn – Cassiel
Sensible, Stubborn

Aquarius – Uriel
Independent, Free thinker

Pisces – Sandalphon
Compassionate, Artistic

Angels of the Moon

There are 28 Angels who rule each day of the 28-day cycle of the phases of the Moon.

1 Geniel	8 Amnediel	15 Atliel	22 Geliel
2 Enediel	9 Barbiel	16 Azeruel	23 Requiel
3 Aniuxiel	10 Ardifiel	17 Adriel	24 Abrinael
4 Azariel	11 Neciel	18 Egibiel	25 Aziel
5 Gabriel	12 Abdizuel	19 Amutiel	26 Tagriel
6 Dirachiel	13 Jazeriel	20 Kyriel	27 Atheniel
7 Schliel	14 Ergediel	21 Bethnael	28 Amnixiel

Angels Governing the 12 Months of the Year

January Gabriel

February Barchiel

March Machidiel

April Ashmodel

May Ambriel

June Muriel

July Verchiel

August Hamaliel

September Uriel

October Barbiel

November Adnachiel

December Anael

Index

Dedicated to Benjamin Brockman

I would like to thank my mother, Lily, and my late father, Sidney Abraham Pepper, for inspiring my spiritual development. I also thank my husband, Jeffrey, for his support, and my children, Nicole, Simone, and Alexis.

Picture credits

Akg Images
p.13, top; p. 39, p. 67, p.77, full page; p.98, full page; p.110, top left; p.151, top right; p.154, full page

Alinari Archives
p.117, top

The Art Archive
p.25, full page

The Bridgeman Art Library
p.7, full page; p.8, full page; p.21, top; p.36, full page; p.41, top right; p.50, full page; p.58, full page; p.72, full page; p.81, full page; p.87, right; p.100, top right; p.103, full page; p.125, full page; p.31, full page; p. 134; p.141, top left; p.148, top left

Sotheby's Picture Library
p.43, bottom; p.108, bottom

Tate images
p.39, top; p.40, bottom